THE KEYS
to Assessing
Language Performance

A teacher's manual
for measuring student progress

PAUL SANDROCK

The American Council on the Teaching of Foreign Languages
1001 North Fairfax Street, Suite 200
Alexandria, VA 22314

Graphic Design by Goulah Design Group, Inc.
Edited by Sandy Cutshall, Print Management, Inc.

© 2010 by The American Council on the Teaching of Foreign Languages, Alexandria, VA

ISBN: 978-0-9705798-3-6

Foreword

Readers will no doubt be drawn to this manual because of its declared focus on measuring student progress. While the emphasis is on assessment of language performance, the first chapter title ("Constructing a Road Map for Teaching and Learning") signals a broader purpose. Indeed, this book is as much about *enhancing* teaching and *improving* learning as it is about evaluation. Accordingly, it reminds us that assessment can function as more than something we do at the end of an instructional segment to obtain a grade. Assessment can, and should, guide curriculum planning, help establish clear performance targets for teaching and learning, and provide helpful feedback for adjustment and improvement.

This manual addresses various aspects of assessment determining appropriate standards-based evidence, designing authentic language tasks and accompanying rubrics, and using performance assessments to engage learners and focus instruction. While each chapter reflects sound principles of assessment, the book does not dwell on theory. Instead, the emphasis is pragmatic, with suggestions and examples linked to daily practice.

This guide would be worth reading if it simply concentrated on summative assessments *of* learning. But Paul Sandrock goes further in exploring the rich terrain of assessing *for* learning and suggesting practical ways in which formative (ongoing) assessments can inform teaching and learning. He offers tried-and-true, manageable methods by which language teachers can use assessments to enhance, as well as evaluate, the performance of their students.

Your work will surely benefit from this resource, and your students will thank you for taking its message to heart.

Jay McTighe
Educational consultant and co-author of *Assessing Learning in the Classroom* (NEA, 1995), *Understanding by Design* (ASCD, 1998, 2005) and *Scoring Rubrics in the Classroom* (Corwin Press, 2000)

Acknowledgments

I want to begin by acknowledging the participants in every workshop I have ever led, because through them I have continued to learn, by exploring ideas around assessment, trying out activities to develop understanding, and identifying effective classroom applications. What I learned with workshop participants formed the basis for this book. This publication is designed to be a resource for classroom teachers, to empower them to develop assessments that are meaningful: meaningful to teachers as feedback on the impact of their instruction and meaningful to students as feedback on their growing ability to use their new language. Thank you to all the teachers who have taught me the impact of performance assessment for learning languages.

My journey in performance assessment has had many milestones. The Integrated Performance Assessment (IPA) project through ACTFL nurtured many of my developing ideas. I appreciate the expertise and collegial support of the project team, and I want to express my deep thanks to Bonnie Adair-Hauck (University of Pittsburgh), Eileen Glisan (Indiana University of Pennsylvania), Keiko Koda (University of Pittsburgh), and Elvira Swender (ACTFL). Through this project and these educators, I learned about the strong research base undergirding performance assessment, research that has been documented and described in other publications. Some key elements are identified in the References section of this book as well as in the research summaries at the beginning of several key chapters. I am very grateful to Judith Shrum and Eileen Glisan for the thorough research base provided in their publication, *Teacher's Handbook: Contextualized Language Instruction* (2005). The majority of the research references summarized for Chapters 3–6 came from the Shrum and Glisan handbook, as well as from Grant Wiggins and Jay McTighe's foundational work, *Understanding by Design* (2005).

Thank you also to the reviewers of this book, many of whom were part of the IPA project, for providing detailed comments and improvements: Bonnie Adair-Hauck, Eileen Glisan, Elvira Swender, Richard Donato (University of Pittsburgh), and Laura Terrill (consultant). Thanks also to Frank "Pete" Brooks (Indiana University of Pennsylvania), for his review of this book and insights into the research base of the material presented. Special acknowledgment goes to ACTFL staff Steve Ackley and Marty Abbott for coaching me throughout the writing process.

Professional organizations are essential to counteract the potential isolation of a classroom. I am very grateful to four groups in particular for involving me through workshops, presentations, and projects that shaped this book. Wisconsin educators, through the Wisconsin Association for Language Teachers, created professional development around standards and assessment. The National Council of State Supervisors for Languages developed LinguaFolio for the United States, a portfolio to document student progress in learning languages. The National Association of District

Supervisors of Foreign Languages spearheaded training to develop teachers' skills in performance assessment. ACTFL developed several projects to translate research into practice, with the goal of improving language teaching and learning.

I thank numerous educators who have kept assessment front and center in my work. So many professional colleagues helped me grow by asking tough questions and posing real scenarios around assessing language performance. Many of these wonderful teachers will recognize their influence throughout this book. Over the years, these peer mentors and I have discussed guiding principles around assessment, co-developed workshop materials, and shared examples to make all of this real. I must give special mention to several colleagues with whom I have collaborated frequently in a variety of ways. I am particularly grateful to:

Marty Abbott, Peggy Boyles, Rita Oleksak, Martin Smith, and Laura Terrill for being mentors around assessment in my journey as a teacher

Carol Commodore, who has shared with me numerous ideas on assessment

Helena Curtain and Carol Ann Dahlberg, whose influence on my thinking has been significant

Donna Clementi, who keeps challenging me to learn and improve through the countless presentations and workshops we have developed together

Finally, I thank my wife, Jean, for making it possible for me to take the time to complete this work, reacting as I tried out ideas to see if they make sense in the classroom, and believing that this is worth sharing.

Paul Sandrock

Table of Contents

Chapter 5: Engaging, Motivating, and Involving Students 67

Chapter 6: Impacting Instruction and Program Articulation Through
Performance Assessments 77

Figures

References

Appendixes

Chapter 1: Constructing a Road Map for Teaching and Learning

"Does this count?" "Is this going to be on the test?" Students constantly ask these questions. Why? They want to know how their teacher is going to evaluate them. They want to know the real goals of the day's lesson and the course. These are certainly reasonable requests, but how can a teacher answer these questions in a way that will shape student learning and focus teaching on what really matters? This book is designed to guide the user through thoughtful steps necessary to develop performance assessments and effective rubrics so teachers can answer these student questions.

Students are not alone in asking such questions. Since the 1990s with the beginning of the national discussion of standards, the American public has intertwined standards with a scrutiny of assessment to determine if students are measuring up: if students are achieving those standards. The notion of accountability has become integrated with the identification of what students should know and be able to do. Assessment is at the heart of the public conversation to improve student achievement.

Language teachers, however, express frustration with assessments that emphasize only low-level recall of vocabulary, manipulation of grammatical structures by filling in blanks, and other substitutions for real communication. When they look at ways to measure student use of language, the main criterion often becomes grammatical accuracy, which relegates language use to a focus on form. The transition to performance assessment focuses both students and teachers on communication. The message that is being communicated becomes the critical component rather than grammatical accuracy, keeping in mind that perfect accuracy is a lifelong goal.

Why do we assess our students? Educators want to use assessment to inform instruction and to provide feedback that will help students improve. Traditionally, educators have used assessment to find out what students have and have not learned, presented as letter grades or numerical scores to later calculate quarter or semester grades. Teachers constantly struggle to balance using assessment to capture and describe the past (i.e., what students have learned) and using assessment to shape the future (i.e., setting goals for improvement).

A coherent and transparent system of assessment and evaluation is required to focus both teachers and students on appropriate program goals and outcomes. Through step-by-step guidance and examples, this book will demonstrate how to design performance assessments that capture language samples in which students are motivated to use language to accomplish real purposes. Next, this guide will detail a process to design rubrics that focus on those aspects which truly help improve student language proficiency. Teachers and students alike can benefit from this road map for teaching and learning.

Why Develop Performance Assessments?

Assessment is a tool. To develop effective assessments, teachers need to ask:

- Why am I assessing my students?
- What information do I hope to learn through this assessment?
- What do I plan to do with the information gained through this assessment?

Answering these questions will set the teacher on a course of matching the need for and use of the information with the right assessment mechanism. Different assessment strategies are needed for different purposes.

If the answers to these three questions identify the goal of assessment as measuring student use of language in real-life situations, then the assessment mechanism must come as close as possible to that authentic use. Performance assessments ask students to use language for real purposes: sharing new information, exchanging opinions, presenting ideas to a specific audience, preparing a letter of application or introduction, understanding the point of view of a speaker or author and comparing it to one's own, or skimming a website to find needed information. A well-designed performance assessment task will generate these genuine acts of communication. The teacher then can focus on what really counts by providing feedback to students based on this evidence of their authentic use of language. Students will know much more than how well they did on a test: They will know how well they can perform when actual communication is needed.

A Balanced System of Assessment: Match Assessment Strategies to Their Purpose

Assessment is an ever-flowing stream of information for teachers and students. Teachers need to consciously develop a continuum of assessment that provides students with everything from specific and highly focused feedback to very broad and holistic feedback. In a balanced assessment system, teachers use both formative and summative levels of assessment.

Paul Black and Dylan Wiliam examined more than 250 studies on formative assessment and summarized its impact in the article "Inside the Black Box: Raising Standards Through Classroom Assessment."[1] They defined formative assessment as "all of those activities undertaken by teachers—and by their students in assessing themselves—that provide information to be used as feedback to modify teaching and learning activities. Such assessment becomes formative assessment when the evidence is actually used to adapt the teaching to meet student needs." James Popham[2] further described formative assessment as "a planned process in which teachers or students use assessment-based evidence to adjust what they are currently doing."

Formative assessment may provide quick learning checks to find out if students have learned and can use specific language elements, usually vocabulary or grammar. As a unit of instruction unfolds, teachers also use formative assessment to help students feel confident that they can begin to manipulate in more meaningful ways the elements first evaluated in fairly concrete ways. Susan Brookhart[3] contrasted formative and summative assessment in this way: "Formative assessment means information gathered and reported for use in the development of knowledge and skills, and summative assessment means information gathered and reported for use in judging the outcome of that development." Formative assessments lead to summative performance assessments and demonstrate to the teacher that students are ready to pull everything together in a real task.

Summative assessment inspires greater confidence, as students demonstrate to themselves and their teacher that they can apply the lessons learned, the skills acquired, and the knowledge gained. This is when students rely on what they have learned, without any scaffolding from the teacher, and show what they are able to do as a result of the instruction. Summative performance assessments present students with a new application of the skills previously assessed at the formative level.

No single assessment instrument or single moment of assessment alone is sufficient to provide students and teachers with all the information needed to identify what to do next. The rich and balanced pool of evidence that is collected to match each specific assessment purpose will guide students in their language learning and teachers in their coaching of that journey. Educators want to make sure that some of that assessment provides evidence of the real performance that is the ultimate instructional goal. Realistically, a teacher cannot evaluate students by dropping them off in a country where the language is spoken to see if they survive. Using performance assessment is the best way to produce students who are ready and confident in their ability to use the language to interact within the target culture.

Link Standards Through Assessment to Curriculum and Instruction

Measuring student performance must start with identifying the target. To ensure that the assessment is not focused only on vocabulary elements or grammatical structures, planning must begin with the standards for learning languages (see Appendix A). Immediately then the focus is on communication and a meaningful context. In national and state standards, language is described by the goal behind the communication: Is it interpretive, interpersonal, or presentational? Viewed from the angle of this communicative purpose, the design of the assessment and the criteria for evaluation become clearer. Both the task and the instrument used for evaluation must fit the communicative purpose. This backward design, beginning with the end in mind, is critical for creating performance assessment tasks.

Once identified, the performance assessments become the filter for selecting the content for teaching. Now teachers have a way to make critical instructional decisions such as how much of a grammatical structure is needed in order to be successful in the assessment task; what vocabulary is essential to learn, which words might be important for passive recognition, and which do not need attention because students will have context and visual clues to figure out their meaning; and the level of accuracy needed for success.

By designing backwards—from standards to specific assessment tasks to the evaluation criteria—the teacher is developing a road map for both teaching and learning. By capturing the true goals for instruction (i.e., a detailed description of what students are actually expected to do as a result of the instruction), the teacher is ready to target the unit and daily lesson plans and to help students know what they are supposed to learn and why.

Identifying and sharing the performance assessment tasks at the beginning of a unit, rather than keeping the assessment a mystery (as in traditional end-of-chapter tests), provides focus and motivation. If the teacher keeps the target clearly in mind throughout the preparation of a unit and the daily teaching plans, logically the students will benefit because each activity, each interaction, each question, and each learning check will be focused on what the students need in order to be successful in that assessment task. Knowing the target, students and teachers will collaboratively and jointly focus on meeting it, thus increasing their chances of hitting that target.

Use Performance Assessments to Provide Useful Feedback and Motivation for Students

Not only do targets guide instruction, they also guide students in their efforts. Rather than guessing what might be on the test, students who know up front how they will be expected to demonstrate what they have learned will get more out of each class period. Students will know what they need to learn from each activity, how well they need to be able to do something, and the language elements that are needed to be successful.

Motivation also comes from the evaluation itself. Well-constructed rubrics describe the expected performance. When students receive feedback on a performance, they know which qualities they demonstrated strongly, which qualities were present only marginally, and which qualities were missing. This targeted feedback assists students in identifying what they need to do to improve, building responsibility for their own learning.

Gauge Student Progress Along the K–12 Performance Guidelines

The ACTFL Performance Guidelines for K–12 Learners outline specific targets along a continuum described through the standards for communication: interpersonal, interpretive, and presentational. The continuum has three benchmarks: Novice, Intermediate, and Pre-Advanced. These benchmarks cover the progress that students learning the same language in K–12 programs typically achieve. The step-by-step process in this book will keep directing the teacher back to the K–12 performance guidelines to make sure the performance assessment tasks and evaluation rubrics are hitting the targeted level of proficiency. Using this continuum puts a wider range of performance in front of the teacher so that all students will be appropriately challenged to grow in their confident use of language. Performance assessments and rubrics then focus on what students will need to do to improve to reach the targeted level or to move to the next level.

Assessment plays a critical role in language education: to help students learn to use their new language, to help teachers focus their instruction to maximize its effectiveness, and to provide the public with the evidence it needs to enthusiastically support language programs. Clearly, assessment is at the heart of the discussion around improving student ability to use the language. With such high stakes, assessment must showcase the performances that are at the heart of proficient use of the language. Performance assessment clarifies the goals and provides critical feedback to students as they seek to mark their progress and improve their performance.

Examples from the IPA Project

ACTFL developed a project to design a process for teachers to integrate performance assessment into their units of instruction. Guiding principles, implementation ideas, and examples from the Integrated Performance Assessment (IPA) project, described in Chapter 2, are woven throughout this book. Lessons learned from the project have been incorporated into the steps outlined here for designing performance assessment tasks.

Chapter 2: | Basing Assessment on Standards

At some point in time, most language instructors teach a unit focused on travel. Whether the unit is focused on getting ready to go on a trip or being in a country where the target language is spoken, many teachers identify a list of specific vocabulary and grammar, such as:

- Airplane vocabulary
- Telling time and dates
- Hotel reservation vocabulary
- Giving and getting directions
- Polite commands
- How to use the train system
- Food
- Ordering in a restaurant

Traditionally, language teachers have been given lists of vocabulary and grammatical structures, similar to this list, that form the basis of their teaching. The challenge is knowing when to stop. How much do students need to know? How many food items do students need to memorize? How much about command forms do they need to know? How many different ways to tell time do they need?

What is not provided in a traditional curriculum is the filter for making decisions as to which words need to be ready as active vocabulary available and able to be produced instantaneously, which words need to be recognized and passively available, and which words are optional for students to use individually. What is not provided is how much of a grammatical structure students need in a given unit to improve their language proficiency and which language functions they need to master and how well. The only way to provide such a filter is to identify the final assessment performance that students are to demonstrate—a performance linked to authentic applications in the real world.

Consider instead that the students are actually getting ready to go on a real trip. What do they need to do and how can they go about doing it? The list would be very different from a random list of vocabulary and grammar topics. It would likely include the following types of actions:

- Go online to check out hotels and flights. Read advice on how to use an ATM machine in the destination country. Browse websites and travel reviews for suggestions of what to do.
- Talk to people who have been there, probing their experiences and advice. Discuss with experienced travelers the advantages and disadvantages of relying on a credit card or using ATMs while abroad.
- Create and write up your itinerary based on your interests. Write to the consulate's information center to discover interesting things to do.

This list instantly answers the questions of how much to teach, when to stop, and what is to be active versus passive vocabulary. These actions suggest the grammatical structures and language functions one will use in preparing for a trip. This list also reflects the three modes of communication in the national standards for learning languages: interpretive, interpersonal, and presentational. Going online and reading reviews are examples of the interpretive mode; talking and discussing are interpersonal; and writing to the consulate is presentational. How well students will do these tasks depends on their current language level and what the teacher is coaching them to be able to do.

Starting with the standards, with the ends in mind, turns traditional unit planning upside down. Prior to the standards era, curriculum consisted of lists of vocabulary and grammar topics. The hope was that if the sequence were correctly arranged, students would develop fluency in the target language. Unit planning started by teaching vocabulary, testing it with a vocabulary quiz, teaching a grammatical structure, testing it with a fill-in-the-blanks worksheet, going back and practicing or drilling more because students were not successful on the tests, realizing that the unit was coming to an end and some culture should be included, and then figuring out what the final test for the unit would be. When the unit test was given, students and teachers were all happy to move on to a new unit.

With the standards as the beginning point, the learning targets are identified up front, as is the way that those targets will be assessed. Once the goals are known, all instructional decisions are derived from them. The assessment drives the instruction. The assessment helps the teacher identify the specific vocabulary and grammatical structures that students will need to be successful. If students are going to show their learning by engaging in a conversation in which they ask each other questions, the teacher needs to identify and teach the forms and vocabulary the students will actually use.

Key Lessons Learned for Designing Performance Assessment Tasks

- Focus the tasks within the context of a unit of instruction
- Identify learning outcomes by starting with standards
- Target the language level

Integrated Performance Assessment Project

After the national standards and K–12 performance guidelines appeared, teachers began to struggle with how to link the two in a meaningful way to guide their instruction. In 1998, ACTFL developed a proposal and received grant funding to design such a link. The Integrated Performance Assessment (IPA) project[1], funded under a grant from the U.S. Department of Education, International Research and Studies Program, provides a model for helping teachers evaluate student development of the knowledge and skills detailed in the standards for learning languages while also making progress in proficiency. The project developers also wanted to provide teachers with useful rubrics for giving students feedback on their performance in order to target areas for improvement.

With those goals in mind, the project developers worked with six pilot sites across the United States and covering grades K–12, in small, medium, and large schools in both urban and non-urban communities. Teachers of Chinese, French, German, Japanese, Latin, and Spanish piloted the assessments. The project developers collected and reviewed the student work, collected written student and teacher reflections, and conducted onsite visits and discussion. The assessments were developed to meet the following criteria.

Characteristics of Integrated Performance Assessment

Authentic: Reflect tasks that individuals do in the world outside the classroom

Performance-based: Reflect how students *use* the language and cultural knowledge in communicative tasks

Based on the three modes of communication: Interpretive, interpersonal, presentational

Integrated: Blend communication with other goal area(s) of the standards

---

Key References

Standards for Foreign Language Learning

A coalition of national professional organizations of language educators developed national content standards to identify what students should know and be able to do as they learn languages in K–16 programs. The standards describe five key goal areas: communication, cultures, connections, comparisons, and communities (i.e., "the 5 Cs"). The overarching goal is "knowing how, when, and why to say what to whom." The standards are found in Appendix A.

National Standards in Foreign Language Education Project. (2006). *Standards for foreign language learning in the 21st century.* Lawrence, KS: Allen Press, Inc.

ACTFL Performance Guidelines for K–12 Learners

Following the development of the national standards, ACTFL organized a project to provide descriptions of proficiency levels for each of the three modes of communication described in the national standards (interpretive, interpersonal, and presentational). The guidelines were based on the *ACTFL Proficiency Guidelines*, but were designed to reflect language learners from kindergarten through senior high. The descriptions provide classroom teachers with a realistic expectation of how students can use language in a performance assessment. The guidelines are found in Appendix B.

ACTFL performance guidelines for K–12 Learners. (1998). Yonkers, NY: The American Council on the Teaching of Foreign Languages.

Show developmental progress of proficiency:

- Novice (Novice-High; beginning)
- Intermediate (Intermediate-Low/Mid; emerging)
- Pre-Advanced (Intermediate-High; expanding)

Blend with classroom instruction and experiences: Teaching to the test (in a positive sense)

The assessments were designed to be integrated; that is, one assessment would provide students with knowledge, content, and experience upon which the next assessment would build, sticking with the same thematic focus through tasks that elicited performances in each of the three modes of communication. The focus was not on discrete learning checks, nor on scaffolded interim assessments, but rather on summative, end-of-unit demonstrations of what students could truly do on their own, within an authentic context that was sustained across an interpretive task, an interpersonal task, and a presentational task.

This model was tested and improved upon through the input and experiences of the pilot teachers. Since the project was completed in 2001, other districts and sites have developed their own integrated performance assessments and contributed to the improvement of the process to develop them.

Structure of the Integrated Performance Assessment

The ACTFL Integrated Performance Assessment consists of a series of tasks at each of three levels—Novice Learner, Intermediate Learner, Pre-Advanced Learner—as defined in the *ACTFL Performance Guidelines for K–12 Learners*. Figure 1 depicts the framework of each IPA.

Overview of Task

Each IPA begins with a general introduction that describes for the student the context for and the purpose of the series of authentic tasks. This introduction provides a framework for the assessment and illustrates how each task is integrated into the next and leads up to the culminating task, which results in an oral or written product (see examples in boxes on the next two pages).

**Figure 1. Performance Assessment Units:
A Cyclical Approach**

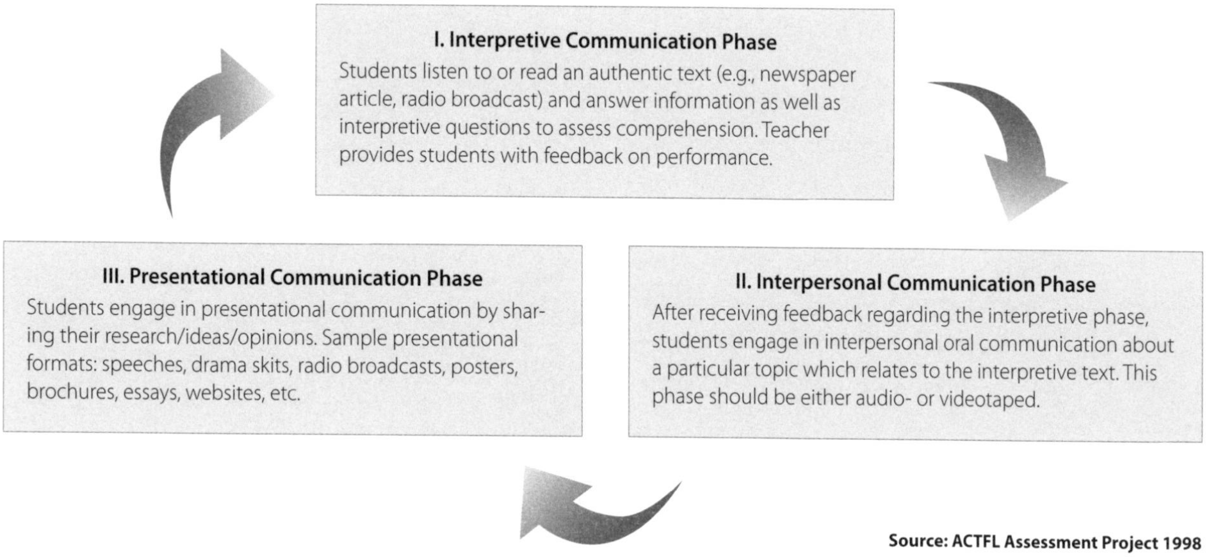

I. Interpretive Communication Phase
Students listen to or read an authentic text (e.g., newspaper article, radio broadcast) and answer information as well as interpretive questions to assess comprehension. Teacher provides students with feedback on performance.

III. Presentational Communication Phase
Students engage in presentational communication by sharing their research/ideas/opinions. Sample presentational formats: speeches, drama skits, radio broadcasts, posters, brochures, essays, websites, etc.

II. Interpersonal Communication Phase
After receiving feedback regarding the interpretive phase, students engage in interpersonal oral communication about a particular topic which relates to the interpretive text. This phase should be either audio- or videotaped.

Source: ACTFL Assessment Project 1998

Note: This chapter reproduces material directly from the Integrated Performance Assessment Manual. See Endnotes on p. 87 for page numbers.

Glisan, E., Adair-Hauck, B., Koda, K., Sandrock, P., & Swender, E. (2003). *ACTFL integrated performance assessment*. Alexandria, VA: The American Council on the Teaching of Foreign Languages.

Example from the IPA Project

"Your Health" Task—Intermediate Level

You have been given the opportunity of a lifetime to attend an athletic training camp in _____ tuition free! This camp trains young people in all sports from the extreme (snowboarding, bicycle motocross, roller blading) to team sports of all kinds (basketball to volleyball). You name it, they help you train for it! To be accepted into the camp, all applicants must convince the admissions office that they have good exercise and nutrition habits. First, you will read about health and nutrition from the perspective of the _____-speaking world. Then you will discuss your eating and exercise regimen with your partner to compare your nutrition and exercise—perhaps, even get some ideas. You will then write your application letter to the summer camp describing your nutrition and training regimen, convincing them that you are well-prepared for the camp and need to be accepted.

Interpretive Tasks

Interpretive tasks include receptive activities such as listening to a news broadcast or radio commercials; reading an article in a magazine, a short story, or a letter; and viewing a film.

In each IPA, students read or listen to an authentic text related to the theme of the IPA. Students complete the interpretive task in the form of a "comprehension guide." This guide assesses the targeted level of performance (Novice, Intermediate, Pre-Advanced) as defined in the *ACTFL Performance Guidelines for K–12 Learners*. The information acquired in the interpretive task is necessary in order for students to be able to complete the interpersonal task in the box. [For sample templates, see Appendix C.]

Example from the IPA Project

"Your Health" Interpretive Task—Intermediate Level

You will read about health and nutrition from the perspective of the _____ -speaking world. Read the article and complete the accompanying "Comprehension Guide."

Interpersonal Tasks

Interpersonal tasks are two-way, interactive activities, such as face-to-face or telephone conversations and spontaneous written correspondence, such as e-mails or text messaging. In oral interpersonal communication, speakers communicate in a spontaneous manner and do not use a written script.

In each IPA, students exchange information with one another, and express feelings, emotions, and opinions about the theme. Each of the two speakers comes to the task with information that the other person may not have, thereby creating a real need for students to provide and obtain information through the active negotiation of meaning. The information gathered during the interpersonal task is necessary to complete the presentational task in the box.

Example from the IPA Project

"Your Health" Interpersonal Task—Intermediate Level

You are quite confident that you are going to be accepted into the athletic camp. Interview a classmate to discuss your eating and exercise regimens. Compare your nutrition and exercise practices—perhaps, even get some ideas.

When the videotape begins, say your first name. Talk with your partner about the regimens you both follow. Ask for examples of what your partner has done in the past month. During your conversation, see how much you both have in common and decide if there are any new habits you can adopt. You will have five minutes.

Note: Students do not read any written notes during the interpersonal task. The interpersonal task is a spontaneous two-way interaction.

Presentational Tasks

Presentational tasks are generally formal speaking or writing activities involving one-way communication to an audience of listeners or readers, such as giving a speech or report, preparing a paper or story, or producing a newscast or video.

In the IPA, students prepare a written or oral presentation based on the topic and information obtained in the previous two tasks. The written or spoken presentational tasks reflect what students would do in the world outside of the classroom. The intended audience includes someone other than the teacher, and the task avoids being merely an opportunity to display language for the teacher. The presentational task is the culminating activity that results in the creation of a written or oral product.

Example from the IPA Project

"Your Health" Presentational Task—Intermediate Level

One requirement for selection to the sports training camp is writing a convincing application letter. Write your application letter to the camp using your research, as well as the findings gathered from your discussion with a classmate. Try to include stories of what you do and have done in the past to keep yourself in the best shape for your sport. Do your best to convince the admissions office that you are more than prepared for the type of training that is offered at the camp.

Teaching to the Assessment: A Middle School Example

Consider a middle school teacher who uses a "backward design" model to plan for instruction. The teacher first determines what she wants her students to be able to do with the target language (in this case, create with language as well as ask and answer questions on a limited variety of topics related to school life, home, and family). This teacher then consults the standards and the district's curriculum to identify and choose the appropriate learning scenarios, themes, and content. Then the teacher maps out and designs an assessment using the IPA template. Once the assessment has been identified and designed, the teacher designs the learning scenarios. The teacher plans the instructional activities in which the students will engage to practice and use the language structures, vocabulary, and communication strategies necessary for the performance task.

Grant Wiggins and Jay McTighe, in their book *Understanding by Design*,[2] would say that this teacher thinks first like an assessor, then like a curriculum designer, and finally like an activ-

ity designer. The outcomes and expectations for students are first and foremost in the teacher's mind before designing the curriculum. Rather than just planning to use different activities at random in the hope that students reach the set goals, this teacher plans a logical progression of tasks and activities. The end result is a unit or series of lessons which are much more meaningful for both students and teacher.

Before students are asked to perform an IPA, this middle school teacher provides them with samples or models of student performance at various levels—"Exceeds Expectations," "Meets Expectations," and "Does Not Meet Expectations." The teacher also provides the rubrics to explain why a student's performance is rated at a particular level. After the modeling phase, students are given opportunities to practice tasks that are similar to IPA tasks. Students evaluate one another's practice performance using the same rubric that will be used as part of the actual IPA. In this way, instruction anticipates and reflects the performance assessment.

When it is time to administer the actual IPA, either for instructional purposes or as an evaluation tool, students read an authentic article and perform the interpretive task, and the teacher provides quality feedback by discussing with students why their interpretive skills are rated "Exceeds," "Meets," or "Does Not Meet" expectations. Through the use of assisting questions and collaborative dialogue, the teacher assists students in understanding the strengths and weaknesses of their performances and, therefore, understanding how to improve their performances on future interpretive tasks.

The teacher then elicits from students the strategies they used to help them with the various stages of listening, reading, or viewing—vocalizing, visualizing, and analyzing word parts, as well as drawing upon their background knowledge. The students are also encouraged to share particular difficulties they experienced and to reflect on possible sources of difficulties encountered (lack of vocabulary, limited comprehension speed, insufficient topic familiarity) in order to promote self-diagnosis and regulation. This feedback loop assists those students who did not fully comprehend the article to understand pertinent information and content before moving into the next phase of the IPA. In this way, the information gleaned from the interpretive phase and the feedback phase assists students with their performance for the next phase of the IPA.

Modeling of Expected Student Performance

Before students begin a task, the teacher and students view samples of exemplary student work and discuss the criteria stated in the rubrics that determine what constitutes performance at each level: "Exceeds Expectations," "Meets Expectations," "Does Not Meet Expectations" (i.e., not there yet). If appropriate, students may also view actual authentic samples of language in the target language.

Students are asked what they think constitutes a good assessment. The teacher elicits student ideas of clear communication and accuracy for their level. The teacher engages in a dialogue with students highlighting the ideas generated by the class. The teacher guides the students into seeing that their ideas match the rubrics. Afterward, the teacher gives the students the ACTFL IPA Rubrics and the *ACTFL Performance Guidelines for K–12 Learners* to show them that they are in very close agreement.

Students are shown anonymous past student work and use a few domains from the rubrics to assess the work. The teacher compares his/her rating of the work with the student rating. (Comprehensibility and vocabulary are usually appropriate domains that the students can help identify.) The teacher also reviews the levels of "Exceeds Expectations," "Meets Expectations," and "Does Not Meet Expectations," so that students have a clear idea of what is expected of them and how they will be assessed. Following the assessment tasks, student performance is scored using rubrics. The ACTFL IPA Rubrics reflect the language and spirit of *The ACTFL Performance Guidelines for K–12 Learners*.[3] Each domain of the performance guidelines is evident in the rubrics. [See Appendix D.]

Implementation of Integrated Performance Assessments

The Integrated Performance Assessment model provides maximum opportunities for language learners to practice using the language in a variety of real-world situations. The IPA is designed to be integrated into classroom instruction and activities by means of the unit or theme being addressed. For example, the "Your Health" IPA fits well within the theme of "food and nutrition," and a "Famous Person" IPA can be integrated within the theme of "description of people." The teacher should provide ample practice of the types of activities present in the IPA. For example, classroom practice that leads up to the "Your Health" IPA might include the following scenario:

> For a Novice-level unit on health and nutrition, students learn about various elements related to health. They read straightforward authentic magazine articles that offer advice for eating healthy foods and discuss the main ideas. They talk about nutrition and the variety of foods that they eat or do not eat. They discuss poor eating habits that they might have, like eating junk food or drinking too many soft drinks. Students make lists (using graphic organizers) of what they eat each week, in a written logbook. The teacher guides the students and provides them with the appropriate language and grammar they need to communicate their messages. Students then compile and share what they eat and the results are posted on a large timeline graph in the classroom. Students might categorize and label the foods that could be considered "healthy" and "unhealthy." They practice role-plays as dieticians or athletic trainers giving advice on healthy eating. They debate their choices and express their own meanings and opinions, using language structures and memorized phrases.

Such classroom practice integrates the three modes of communication within the specific thematic focus and leads naturally to the use of the IPA as a culminating assessment.

Chapter 3: Step-by-Step: Designing Performance Assessment Tasks

Seven Steps for Designing Performance Assessment Tasks

1. Create a rich and engaging thematic focus

2. Identify what students need to do to demonstrate their learning

3. Evaluate tasks against the targeted level of proficiency

4. Sort performance tasks as formative or summative

5. Fine-tune and integrate the summative performance tasks

6. Incorporate other standards to enrich the unit of instruction and performance tasks

7. Pilot with students and use the results to adjust the assessment tasks

Road Map for Teaching and Learning: Backward Design of Performance Assessment Tasks

Measuring student performance must start with identifying the target. To ensure that the assessment is not focused only on vocabulary elements or grammatical structures, the design must begin with what students are expected to do as a result of teaching and learning. Teaching a unit without clear targets in mind is like starting to drive without a road map: You may have a general sense of where you want to go, but you have no idea of how to get there. With a road map, every move is efficiently and effectively moving you toward the target. In teaching, with a road map and with clear end-of-unit assessments, every activity in the classroom will lead toward that target or goal—and the teacher will know when the students have truly learned the knowledge and skills that are the focus of the unit. For learning languages, the target is using a new language to interpret, exchange, and present information and ideas. At a unit level, the target must focus specifically on how students will demonstrate their language skills in that context and at that point in time, such as having Novice-level students plan together advice for a visiting exchange student on how to eat healthy in a U.S. fast food restaurant. Along the "road" to that destination, other milestone targets help focus instruction and learning. For example, students scan restaurant menus to identify items from the various food groups or create a list of what they ate during one day and identify the impact on the body of different items. Like highway signs showing miles remaining to the destination, these milestones help the students know that they are on track to reach their destination.

By designing backwards from standards to specific tasks, the teacher is developing a road map of learning targets for both teaching and learning. Capturing the real goals for instruction in terms of a detailed description of what students actually are expected to do as a result of the instruction gives direction to the unit and daily lesson plans and helps students know what they are supposed to learn and why. Focusing on the target

What Insights on Designing Performance Assessment Tasks Are Implied from Research?

A Meaningful and Communicative Context Supports Learning:

- Adair-Hauck and Cumo-Johanssen (1997) suggest that a whole-language approach helps students acquire language more strongly than a traditional grammar-based approach.
- Toth's study (2004) identifies a more natural conversation focus as stronger than a grammar focus in helping students process what is said.
- Curtain and Dahlberg (2004) emphasize the importance of a thematic center to support comprehension, providing a context to involve students in use of the target language.

Assessing for Understanding Requires Assessing for Transfer:

- Bloom (1956) describes assessment of "application" as requiring a new task, best within a context and a practical usage.
- Wiggins and McTighe (2005) describe understanding as demonstrated when one has to cope with real world challenges in all their ambiguity, rather than by a single cue stimulating a single response.
- Gardner (1991) summarizes research on assessing understanding by stating that if a slight alteration in the test does not lead to a documentation of the competence being assessed, then understanding has not been achieved.

Contextual Support and Cognitive Involvement Are Critical:

- Cummins (1981) supports the use of communicative activities with a strong context and context-embedded language to assist student understanding. Additional support comes from embedding a degree of cognitive involvement through higher-order thinking and a connection with prior learning or with other subject areas.

Lower Anxiety Helps Students Learn the Language:

- Vogely (1998) identified four sources of anxiety in beginning Spanish students during listening tasks, including unfamiliar topics and vocabulary and a lack of visual support.

- Krashen (1982) posits that language acquisition takes place when student anxiety or affective filter is low.

Design of the Task Can Support Development of the Communication Skills:

- Terry (1998) showed that student difficulty in an activity comes from the task itself, not from the nature of the text.
- Villegas Rogers and Medley (1988); and Shrum and Glisan (2005) have shown that authentic texts have a natural form, a cultural and situational context, and serve a purpose.
- Young (1993, 1999) and Vigil (1987) conclude that students show more comprehension on authentic texts than on simplified versions.
- Geddes and White (1978) compare semiscripted text or segments as recorded by native speakers given a situation to role-play, and while they feel semiscripted segments are not authentic, they suggest that they do provide examples of authentic language.
- Adair-Hauck and Cumo-Johanssen (1997) advocate a top-down approach in which students move from guided help to understand the main idea to understanding details.
- Scarcella and Oxford (1992) find that listening involves simultaneously processing bottom-up and top-down. Swaffar, Arens, and Byrnes (1991) suggest the same simultaneous approaches occur in reading comprehension.
- Hammadou Sullivan (2002) identifies the process of making inferences to include generalizing "typical" events and identifying reasons why such events explain the text.
- Researchers have identified viewing as an important element of the interpretive mode, helping students learn grammar (Ramsay, 1991), Advanced-level proficiency skills (Rifkin, 2000), and cultural information (Herron, Corrie, Cole, & Dubreil, 1999).
- Shrum and Glisan (2005) summarize the implications of Swain's work (1985, 1995), encouraging teachers "to provide opportunities for output that is meaningful, purposeful, and motivational so that students can consolidate what they know about the language and discover what they need to learn." (p. 20)

clearly benefits students because each activity, each interaction, each question, and each learning check zeroes in on what the students need in order to be successful at that assessment task. The performance assessment tasks provide focus and motivation, rather than forcing students to guess what might be on the test. When students know up front how they will be ex-

pected to demonstrate what they have learned, they will also know what they need to get out of each activity, how well they need to be able to do something, and the language they need to be successful. Knowing the target, students and teachers will greatly increase their chances to successfully hit it!

Defining Terms

Thematic Focus: Provides "a richer basis for a unit, one that has greater potential for meaning and purpose;"[1] engaging students through "a meaningful topic (e.g., planning a trip to Spain), a subject-content theme (e.g., preserving the environment, healthy foods), or a specific context (e.g., a story or folktale)."[2]

Essential Questions: The questions that "lie at the heart of a subject or curriculum . . . and promote inquiry,"[3] generating "a variety of thoughtful responses"[4] (e.g., What defines a healthy lifestyle? What makes a good travel destination? How do clothes define who you are?), tapping student interests, and providing an overarching focus for the tasks, performances, and outcomes of a unit of instruction.

Context: Defines key elements of the performance: who (participants), what (goals), where (setting), when (in class or not), how (tone, norms of interaction, register), genre (speech, conversation, essay), and why (motive). "The features of context. . . enable speakers and writers to make language choices about what is said, to whom, when, and where."[5]

Language Levels: "The four major levels, or major borders, of performance according to the ACTFL Proficiency Rating Scale, defined in terms of the linguistic, pragmatic, and strategic skills with which the global tasks or functions are accomplished: Novice, Intermediate, Advanced, and Superior. The three major levels of performance according to the *ACTFL Performance Guidelines for K–12 Learners* that describe learner performance across the three modes of communication and along the developmental path that occurs within a school setting: Novice, Intermediate, Pre-Advanced."[6]

Language Functions: Describe communication tasks "that speakers or writers are able to do with language, ranging from simple tasks such as greeting and leave-taking to complex tasks such as describing, narrating, supporting an opinion, and hypothesizing."[7]

Modes of Communication: As described in the *Standards for Foreign Language Learning in the 21st Century*,[8] the three modes of communication "focus on the context and purpose of communication and operate in an integrated fashion in communication."[9] The interpretive mode focuses on interpreting meaning from what is heard, read, or viewed without the opportunity to interact with the initiator of the communication. The interpersonal mode is spontaneous two-way oral or written exchange of ideas or information where those in the conversation actively negotiate meaning. The presentational mode is one-way communication (speaking, writing, or visually presenting) where the receiver does not have an immediate opportunity to negotiate meaning with the "presenter" or ask for clarification.

Formative Assessment: Learning checks, guided activities, applications of skill and knowledge, with more teacher assistance, intervention, and support; "designed to help shape learners' understanding and skills while there is an opportunity for the teacher and learners to work together to bring about further development and improvement."[10]

Summative Assessment: End-of-unit or end-of-course assessment of language performance; a demonstration of what students should be able to do on their own as a result of the unit of instruction.

Designing Performance Assessment Tasks

Step One: Create a Rich and Engaging Thematic Focus

Too often, teachers identify the thematic focus of a unit as not much more than a vocabulary list. Frequently we hear of the "food" unit or a "clothing" unit. At other times, the unit focus is little more than a grammatical structure in disguise, such as a unit on what students will do in the future. To engage students and provide substance to explore throughout a unit of instruction, the thematic focus needs to incorporate an important question to explore.

Identifying a thematic focus may begin with a topic provided in text materials or other available resources. What is important is what students are asked to do within the thematic focus. Students need to be personally engaged with the theme in order to be motivated to perform their best on the assessment tasks.

Grant Wiggins and Jay McTighe refer to essential questions as an important focus in their curriculum design process, *Understanding by Design*.[11] Essential questions engage students in their learning and guide teachers in their teaching. The essential question around which the teacher develops a unit of instruction creates a focus for the class activities. This thematic focus allows for a deeper exploration of the topic and extended practice of the skills needed for that exploration.

The travel unit envisioned in the opening vignette of Chapter 2 becomes more focused on authentic performance goals when one considers how to actually prepare for a trip. The thematic focus of a trip may come right out of the textbook, but the teacher needs to help students create a personal link and focus the questions for exploration. By looking at what students are able to do at a specific stage of their language development, certain questions lend themselves to the type of investigation they can handle at that language level. Examine how these essential questions match the increasingly complex and sophisticated language students are able to use at each level in the charts in this section.

Essential Questions and Language Needed by Level

Proficiency Level	Essential Question	Language Needed to Explore the Essential Question
Novice	Where would I like to travel?	Direct, descriptive language; likes and dislikes; lists
Intermediate	Why would I choose a particular destination?	More extended description
Pre-Advanced	How will travel help my career options?	Presenting a point of view; elaboration
Advanced	How might travel change the way I look at the world?	Presenting an argument; organized points of support; exploring alternative outcomes

To push the essential question into the realm of what will be motivating to students, a meaningful and purposeful context needs to be included. The context should be:
- Cognitively engaging
- Intrinsically interesting
- Culturally connected[12]
- Communicatively purposeful

DOING IT ON YOUR OWN

In these "Doing It on Your Own" boxes, which will follow the description of each of the seven steps for designing performance assessment tasks, a template is provided for your reflection. Thinking about an actual unit of instruction will help you go step-by-step through the process, leading to the development of your own performance assessment tasks.

Step One: Create a Thematic Focus

Original topic (Chapter or Unit):
(Example: Friends)

Vocabulary and grammar focus:
(Example: Adjectives of characteristics; verbs in first and third-person singular)

Targeted language level, functions emphasized in this unit:
(Example: Novice–Describe with lists of adjectives or verbs)

Brainstorm possible topics:
(Example: Qualities of my friends, what I or my friends like to do)

Design the thematic focus through essential questions (Step One):
(Example: What makes a good friend? How am I a good friend to others?)

Unit Level Examples

Original Topic	Language Level	Key Elements of Unit	Essential Questions (Refocus of Unit)
Food	Novice	Healthy food; food pyramids; diet in different cultures	What would I eat in different countries to keep me healthy? How do I choose what to eat?
Food	Intermediate	Healthy food; cultural customs around food; cultural attitudes toward eating	How do we use food for more than nourishment?
Food	Pre-Advanced	Diet and geography; meals as social connectors; attitudes toward food	How is our diet affected by culture, where we live, and our economic status?
Additional Thematic Examples			
Neighborhoods	Novice	Shops; streets; homes	How will I feel comfortable in my neighborhood?
Daily Routines	Novice	Routines; activities; schedules	Describe your busiest day: What makes it busy for you? How would your day be different if you were living in another culture?
Current Events	Intermediate	Internet newspaper sites; current political and economic issues	How is an event reported differently in another culture?
Literature	Pre-Advanced	Short stories; novels; historical, social, or regional background information	How would a piece of literature be different if written in and for a different culture?

Step Two: Identify What Students Need to Do to Demonstrate Their Learning

Take the thematic focus, consider the targeted language level, and determine the various ways that students can demonstrate their learning. Think through the filter of the three modes of communication (interpretive, interpersonal, and presentational) in order to guarantee a balance in designing the unit of instruction. Decide what interpretive, interpersonal, and presentational activities students might do around the thematic focus. Consider things you have used in the past to teach this unit and adapt them to more directly build students' skills in the modes of communication. Envision what students did in the previous unit to demonstrate their level of performance. Then try to both reinforce that level of skill and push students to do more or to do the same things but more independently, with less support from the teacher or the materials. At this point, it is not important if an activity is interpretive, interpersonal, or presentational; simply generate ideas on what students will do with the language in this unit. Consider all three modes of communication to keep these ideas flowing and expanding beyond past activities. The sorting will occur later.

The chart below examines a variety of ways that students might demonstrate their learning in the classroom.

Framework of Assessment Approaches and Methods [13]				
How Might We Assess Student Learning in the Classroom?				
Thematic focus: What makes a good travel destination?				
Selected-Response Format	**Constructed-Response Format**			
	Brief Constructed Response	**Performance-Based Assessment**		
		Product	**Performance**	**Process-Focused Assessment**

• Multiple-choice (Which destinations are found in countries speaking the language?)
• True–false (Statements of what one can do in various destinations)
• Matching (Match where various monuments are located)
• Enhanced multiple-choice (After answering questions on travel destinations by selecting from among the answers provided, select additional details about each destination from a multiple-choice list)
	• Fill-in-the-blank
	  - word(s)
	  - phrase(s)
	• Short answer
	  - sentence(s)
	  - paragraph(s)
	• Label a diagram (Place cities on a map; place monuments in the appropriate region)
	• "Show your work" (Show the calculations used to identify distances apart in order to plan what to do in a day in a location)
	• Visual representation
	  - web
	  - concept map
	  - flow chart
	  - graph/table
	  - illustration
	(Summarize information found on a website by filling in details on a visual representation given with a few elements filled in; students complete the visual representation with information found)
		• Essay
		• Research paper
		• Story/play
		• Poem
		• Portfolio
		• Model
		• Video/audiotape
		
		(All could be ways to showcase what students learned about travel destinations, personalizing what was found and presenting the information to convince others of what makes a "good" destination)
			• Oral presentation
			• Dramatic reading
			• Enactment
			• Debate
			• Teach-a-lesson (Planned presentations to share what was learned about various travel destinations)
				• Oral questioning
				• Interview (Ask and answer questions of one another to defend personal choice of a good travel destination)
				• Conference (Teacher conducts interview of what was learned)
				• "Think aloud" (Conversation with students to find out how they were able to interpret the text read, heard, or viewed)
				• Learning log (Students keep a record of new things learned throughout their exploration of travel destinations)

DOING IT ON YOUR OWN

Step Two: Brainstorm What Students Are to Do

Thematic focus (from Step One):

(Example: What makes a good friend? How am I a good friend to others?)

Targeted language level, functions emphasized in this unit (from Step One):

(Example: Novice–Describe with lists of adjectives or verbs)

Brainstorm possible ways students will demonstrate their learning (Step Two)

(Examples):

- *Ask other students what they like to do.*
- *Ask other students what they do to help others.*
- *In small groups, list characteristics of a good friend.*
- *Tell what good friends do and don't do.*

- *Hear statements and identify if a good friend would or would not do that.*
- *List what friends do in school, what friends do outside of school.*
- *Write down two things you will do to be a better friend to others.*

REFLECTION

Check the learning, practice, and assessment activities in a unit of instruction. Does a balance of the three modes of communication exist? Are students asked to demonstrate some performance of the language?

If not, what might be added to gather more performance-based assessment evidence?

Describe some specific activities that would provide that balance of the three modes of communication and a balance of selected-response, constructed-response, and performance-based assessments.

How can learning activities be potential opportunities for giving students feedback (formative assessments)?

Step Three: Evaluate Tasks Against the Targeted Level of Proficiency

Check on the characteristics of the targeted level of proficiency. Compare the characteristics of the targeted level to the tasks identified in Step Two. Make sure the tasks will elicit that level of performance from students. The chart on the next page summarizes the ACTFL K–12 performance guidelines to provide a quick overview, useful for this step. Compare what you are asking students to do in your unit's various performance tasks with the characteristics of the targeted language level, not merely for an exact match, but also to see if you are providing tasks that will help students move toward the next level. Building student proficiency by helping them be successful in stretching to the next level will allow them to continue to increase their proficiency rather than staying on a plateau.

Summary of K–12 Performance Guidelines

Compare the characteristics of language for the targeted level with what students would produce in the tasks identified in Step Two. To get a sense of the language students would use, utilize the targeted question types to see what level of language the task is likely to generate. For example, if the teacher is targeting a task at the Intermediate-Mid level, but only asks students to make choices or produce lists, then the task is only going to generate Novice-level language from students. The task needs to have students describe something, explain an opinion, or explore another possibility in order to make sure that they used Intermediate-Mid language in doing the task.

Moving from One Proficiency Level to the Next [14]		
Targeted Level	**Characteristics**	**Targeted Question Types**
Novice	Imitates patterns; mimicry; understands the gist; needs familiar context; uses cognates; imitates cultural behaviors; relies on visual clues and repetition; responds to high-frequency cues	Yes/No (Do you like strawberries?) Choices (Do you want coffee or tea?) Information/Fact (What do you want?) Question tag (You want to stay, don't you?) Questions to generate lists (What sports do you like?)
To move to the next level, guide students to do the following: • Name and identify • Begin to use phrases and description		
Intermediate-Low	Begins to recognize linguistic patterns; moves outside memorized context and patterns; loses accuracy; has more pauses and hesitation; understands some supporting ideas; relies on visual support; provides short answers	Polite requests (I'd like to know more about your school; Tell me about why you like tennis.) Series of questions to develop (exhaust) the topic (How many courses are you taking? Which do you like best? Describe your favorite teacher.)
To move to the next level, guide students to do the following: • Recombine memorized phrases • Begin to use sentences and more original phrasing		
Intermediate-Mid	Expresses own thoughts; experiments; needs familiar topics; uses sentences and strings of sentences; responds to unrehearsed questions; uses variety of tenses with some errors; notices errors (oral and written); uses circumlocution	Open-ended requests (Tell me about the tennis team in your school; Why are sports valued in your school or community?) Ask for new possibilities (What other sport might you think about playing? Why?)
To move to the next level, guide students to do the following: • Use more complex thoughts • Apply language in new contexts		
Pre-Advanced	Feels confident in using target language (at ease); discusses wide range of topics; understands supporting details; negotiates to increase comprehension; is independent; analyzes perspectives and applies understanding; sustains use of target language	Polite requests (Can you tell me about what you used to do as a child?) Follow-up questions (It sounds like you were very active as a child. How has your life changed?) Ask for comparisons (Can you compare high school to college?) Develop the topic to complete the story (You said you went to France. What were your first impressions? What is something unusual that happened?)
To move to the next level, guide students to do the following: • Explain and describe fully, building to paragraph-length discourse • Apply language in broad range of contexts		

Sample Activities Matched to Targeted Language Level [15]	
Targeted Language Level	**Activities**
Novice	Meet a friend in the school cafeteria and find out what classes each of you have for the afternoon, looking for anything in common, so you can arrange a quick meeting with another friend.
	To get ready for a visiting exchange student coming to stay with your family, write a letter of introduction, providing basic information about your family to better prepare the visitor.
Intermediate-Low	Meet a friend in the school cafeteria and discuss what you both like best and least about school in order to prepare a sheet of "What to Expect" for visiting exchange students.
	Maintain a conversation for two minutes about what is your busiest day.
Intermediate-Mid	Give a short speech about aspects of your school that make it more than just a place to take classes.
Pre-Advanced	Write an essay comparing and contrasting U.S. and the target cultures' perspectives on an issue, such as the urgency of recycling, finding alternative energy sources, or supporting healthy diets.

A critical step is to look at the characteristics of the targeted language level, along the continuum of Novice to Advanced. Use this frame as a way of evaluating the tasks you identified and to revise the tasks to be the right match.

Language Demands

- Are the tasks set too low, too easy?
- Are the tasks demanding language that is too challenging, too hard?
- Do the tasks ask students to stretch but not to the point of frustration?

Movement from Teacher-Supported to Independent Use of Language

- Are some of the tasks fairly easy and direct, tasks that will help students warm up and get ready for increasingly challenging tasks?
- Is there a continuum that builds student language skills toward more independent language tasks?
- When asked to stretch, do the tasks have scaffolded support to help students stretch successfully?

Teacher Expectations

- Are the more summative tasks open-ended enough to allow students to demonstrate performance *beyond* your expectations, or are you limiting the performance because students are not asked to do more than an *average* performance that will *meet* expectations?
- Are expectations realistic when students are asked to perform without teacher support?

The summative performance assessment tasks will not be as accurate as they are at the formative learning check level, where students only have to remember vocabulary or a single grammatical structure. When students have to bring many elements together, they will often perform with less accuracy. This is to be expected. Students experience higher levels of language production when activities are well supported and structured by the teacher. Eventually independent language performance by students will reach this destination, but it takes many directed experiences before students can use structures independently with accuracy.

Step Three: Check Targeted Proficiency Level

Thematic focus (from Step One):

(Example: What makes a good friend? How am I a good friend to others?)

Targeted language level, functions emphasized in this unit (from Step One):

(Example: Novice–Describe with lists of adjectives or verbs)

Brainstorm possible ways students will demonstrate their learning (Step Two)

(Examples):

- *Ask other students what they like to do.*
- *Ask other students what they do to help others.*
- *In small groups, list characteristics of a good friend.*
- *Tell what good friends do and don't do.*

- *Hear statements and identify if a good friend would or would not do that.*
- *List what friends do in school, what friends do outside of school.*
- *Write down two things you will do to be a better friend to others.*

Description of targeted language level and functions emphasized, to compare with brainstormed tasks (Step Three)

(Example: Novice–Describe with lists of adjectives or verbs)

Revisions to brainstormed tasks (Step Three)

Step Four: Sort Performance Tasks as Formative or Summative

Sort the potential performance tasks into those that are formative and those that are truly summative. In formative assessment, teachers use learning checks, guided activities, and applications of skill and knowledge to measure student progress toward the learning goals. Teachers initially provide more intervention and support, and then gradually reduce the level of assistance so students move toward a more independent performance. In summative assessment, teachers elicit evidence of what students should be able to do on their own as a result of the unit of instruction. Summative assessment in the context of the process described and practiced in this publication needs to capture the learning goals for the unit. Although the summative assessment of different modes of communication often occurs near the end of the unit, these assessments may occur at any point where that goal has been reached in the unit.

At this step, take the list of identified tasks from Step Two and develop the continuum begun in Step Three while examining the language expectations of the tasks. Some of the performance tasks are going to lend themselves well to formative learning checks, where the teacher is trying to quickly gauge student achievement of specific language elements (vocabulary or grammatical structures). Some will be formative checks where students have to use more than a single element, still in controlled ways, but moving toward independent application. Some may be the final summative performance assessment tasks for the unit, and these now need to be developed. In this iterative process, being able to see the continuum of the activities in a unit of instruction makes it easier to create and describe the end goal. Now, too, the teacher can evaluate the balance of the three modes of communication in the unit: Is there sufficient practice and an appropriate assessment target in each of the three modes of communication: interpretive, interpersonal, and presentational?

What Makes a Good Friend? How Am I a Good Friend to Others? Sorted as Formative and Summative Assessment Tasks—Novice Level

Formative

- Ask other students what they like to do.
- Ask other students what they do to help others.
- In small groups, list characteristics of a good friend.
- Hear statements and identify if a good friend would or would not do that.
- List what friends do in school, what friends do outside of school.
- Write down two things you will do to be a better friend to others.

Summative

- Listen to a conversation and on a list of things that good friends do, check off what these friends say they do for each other.
- Identify with a partner what good friends do and don't do.
- Write a letter to a friend identifying three things you plan to do as a good friend and three things you will not do as a good friend.

Formative Versus Summative

Assessment is an ever-flowing stream of information. Not all assessment comes at the end of unit or end of semester. Teachers need to be conscious of providing a balanced assessment system: formative and summative. This continuum of assessment provides students with a stream of feedback. The nature of feedback changes as well, depending on the nature of the assessment:

- In formative assessment, feedback is specific and highly focused, as students are learning and practicing various building blocks in preparation for the final unit level performances (e.g., commenting on pronunciation, use of a specific structure, or ability to elaborate and provide more detail).
- In summative assessment, feedback is more broad and holistic, where the teacher steps back and looks at the overall performance (e.g., commenting on student ability to get meaning across, maintain a conversation, or organize a strong argument).

Formative assessment ranges from quick learning checks to activities guiding students to more independent use of language. The goal is to find out if students have learned specific language elements (usually vocabulary or grammar), comprehension strategies, or communication strategies. Formative assessment also helps students feel confident that they can begin to manipulate language elements in more meaningful ways and begin to have control over key strategies for using language.

One example of feedback to provide in a formative assessment is to use different colored (pink, yellow, and green) sticky notes to indicate the students' degree of success on the formative task, similar to the meaning of a traffic signal. While students are responding during a class activity, the teacher places on each one's desk a green note to indicate a performance meeting expectations (green = "go ahead"), a yellow note to indicate a performance that almost meets expectations, but with a few reservations (yellow = "caution, be alert, proceed slowly"), and a pink note to indicate a performance that does not meet expectations (red/pink = "stop, not ready to proceed"). At the end of the class period, students write their name on their colored note and then place it on the teacher's folder as they leave the classroom, providing an effective formative learning check, which can be recorded to indicate progress over the course of the unit.[16]

In summative assessment, students demonstrate to themselves and their teacher that they can apply the lessons learned, the skills acquired, and the knowledge gained in the unit of instruction. This is when students produce language on their own and show what they are able to do as a result of the instruction. Summative assessment is a new application of the individual elements of vocabulary and grammar assessed at the formative level. Through summative assessment, students showcase the level of proficiency acquired.

Sample Formative Assessments

Ticket to leave: To make sure that each student has learned a key element for the day, the teacher designs a "ticket" to leave, a word or phrase which each student either says to the teacher or writes down and hands to the teacher on exiting class. The ticket could be a summarizing question on vocabulary, such as to tell two ways to say goodbye or write a description of one animal. The ticket could be proof of internalizing a grammatical concept, such as "Tell me to do something"(e.g., give me a piece of paper), or "Write down one thing you did yesterday."

Quick oral checks: As formative assessment, a task can be adjusted to the expanding abilities of the students. Teachers move from yes–no questions (e.g., "Does a good friend help a friend with homework?"), to forced-choice questions (e.g., "When a friend is being bullied, should a good friend step in to fight back, go get help, or escort the friend to where there is an adult?"), and finally to open-ended questions (e.g., "How can a friend be helpful without doing the work for the friend?"). Ask students either–or questions, thus modeling the right answer and structure and allowing the student to identify the correct response and repeat it. Another approach is to have students finish a sentence, where the beginning stem gives a clear indication of what is expected, whether it is a single word or a phrase, (e.g., "Tomorrow you are going to bring to class your . . . " or "When the weather is really cold, before going outside I am going to put on . . . "). Numerous answers can be elicited from students in this way.

Information gap pair activity: To practice interpersonal communication, students need to use the discrete language elements they have learned in a communicative activity: Each student receives a paper with some but not all of the information needed to complete a task. Students then need to communicate with one another, asking and answering questions, problem solving, hypothesizing, and discussing in order to achieve the designated task. In designing the activity, the goal is to motivate students to get engaged in their need to communicate rather than focusing only on the completion of the task. For example, students would provide their own class schedules and be required to find out any teachers they have in common and a time when they both could meet to complete their assignment from that teacher.

Maintain the conversation: Students can practice interpersonal communication by trying to keep the conversation going on a single topic, asking questions and commenting on their partner's responses. Prior to using this for a formative assessment task, the students have practiced providing appropriate comments, such as: "Interesting," "Tell me more," "What happened next?" or "I can't believe that." Students have an envelope of questions related to the topic to pull out when they get stuck. At the end of the time limit, students want to be the partner who pulled out the fewest questions, or the person who best sustained the conversation.

Leave a message: Another formative assessment of interpersonal communication is to have students listen to a prompt or read an e-mail or text message and reply by recording a voice message or sending an e-mail response.

Finding information on the Internet: As an effective formative assessment of interpretive communication, students are given a website or simply a topic to search on their own for a website. The teacher needs to focus the task, making for purposeful skimming and scanning for information.

Write captions: In this formative assessment of presentational communication, students summarize illustrations that tell a story by writing a caption or brief summary for each one.

Finish a story: Another presentational task is to have students read part of a story and tell or write an ending.

Rough draft: Students write a rough draft of an essay, article, or story and receive feedback on organization and mechanics, providing the author with the opportunity to correct errors that may confuse the reader.

Sample Summative Assessments

Interpersonal: Based on the current unit, a pair of students has a specific amount of time to try to accomplish a conversational task. Tasks might include finding out how much they have in common on the topic, coming to agreement on a related issue, or identifying as much as they know together about a topic. The amount of time should be sufficient to gather the language sample, but not so long as to exhaust students' language repertoire. In the IPA project, students produced solid Novice-level language in a two-minute conversation, Intermediate-level language in four- to five-minute conversations, and Pre-Advanced-level language in eight- to 10-minute conversations. Students might be able to continue the conversation beyond these limits, but the language level produced did not change when the time limit extended longer than these suggested times.

Interpretive: Students might be asked to summarize the information found from three different websites to form a more complete response to a question or to provide a summary of a topic. For example, Pre-Advanced students are given websites for newspapers from 10 different countries (in the target language). The task is to identify a national story of importance in the students' hometown newspaper, search for that same story in three different foreign newspapers' websites, and then to compare the level of importance given, the longevity of the story in the foreign press versus the local press (i.e., how many days the story continues to have prominence), and the similarities or differences in the way the story is presented (i.e., any differences in political slant or cultural attitudes).

Presentational: Students organize information and write a postcard or letter to a potential host family or a student to be hosted, using the target language for a meaningful purpose. The teacher targets the tasks to fit the language level, student developmental level, and the current unit of instruction. Example: Intermediate students write a letter to a potential foreign student that their family will be hosting, explaining differences in responsibilities and house rules that could be anticipated, knowing the cultural differences. Novice-level students on an imaginary trip abroad write a postcard back to their language teacher about what they did on the trip, using memorized language, but in new and creative applications.

DOING IT ON YOUR OWN

Step Four: Sort Performance Tasks as Formative and Summative

Thematic focus (from Step One):
(Example: What makes a good friend? How am I a good friend to others?)

Targeted language level, functions emphasized in this unit (verified through Step Three):
(Example: Novice–Describe with lists of adjectives or verbs)

Identify Formative and Summative Tasks—How Students Will Demonstrate Their Learning (Step Four)			
	Interpretive	Interpersonal	Presentational
Formative:			
Summative:			

Step Five: Fine-Tune and Integrate the Summative Performance Tasks

Now it is time to fine-tune the unit-level summative performance tasks and make sure they have been integrated such that one serves as preparation for the next. This provides a content connection, a meaningful context to tie the assessment tasks together. If the tasks are connected, doing one should help students do the next one by providing practice, ideas, and feedback. The tasks do not have to occur three days in a row, nor at the very end of a unit of instruction. Student interest in the assessment tasks rises as does their motivation to do their best, as they see how doing one task helps with the next one.

This connection of one task to the next is at the heart of the IPA project's model:

Figure 2. Shortened Version of IPA Project Model

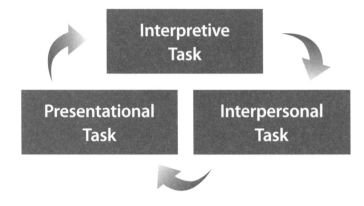

With a skeletal outline of the summative performance tasks for each of the three modes of communication, you can begin to see how to link them. The standards not only provide an appropriate organizing framework for assessment, they provide motivation for students. Students will be much more engaged and excited about learning vocabulary and grammatical structures when they know that they need these elements to successfully use language for interpretive, interpersonal, or presentational purposes. Assessments need to generate this same motivation.

The below examples for the travel unit at various levels illustrate how the first assessment leads to the second, which leads to the third. By doing the first assessment, reviewing it, and reflecting on what was learned, students are better prepared for the second, and then again for the third assessment. This is the integrated nature of performance assessments. There is no magic in the order of the tasks, rather the flow comes from the logical link of needing to do one task before doing the next.

Unit Level Performance Assessments			
What makes the right travel destination for me?			
Level	**Interpretive**	**Presentational**	**Interpersonal**
Novice Where would I like to travel?	Listen to a travelogue: match photos to each description heard.	Write a brief website description for five places of interest (where, hours open, admission, etc.).	In pairs, look at five photos and discuss likes and dislikes, deciding which two places to visit on your last day in the target country.
Intermediate Why would I choose a particular destination?	**Interpretive** Using Internet resources, fill in requested information about the area you have selected to visit in the target country.	**Presentational** Create a commercial and a flyer to promote the region you have selected.	**Interpersonal** Discuss with a partner the places in classmates' commercials, deciding which will be the most exciting to visit and how you will convince the rest of your class.
Pre-Advanced (Intermediate-High) How could travel help my career options?	**Interpretive** Investigate places for study, travel, or work in the target country; identify how they would be helpful to four careers you are exploring.	**Interpersonal** Evaluate with a partner the career advantages you could gain by studying, traveling, or working in the target country.	**Presentational** Write a letter to apply for an internship, explaining how the experience will fit into your career plans, and how you have prepared for it.
Advanced How does travel change the way I look at the world?	**Interpersonal** Discuss stereotypes of the target culture that you know you see differently now; identify ideas you want to investigate while in the target country.	**Presentational** Write a newspaper editorial explaining one U.S. cultural phenomenon that is likely to be misinterpreted by tourists from the target country.	**Interpretive** Read a work of literature with a strong sense of place; describe the cultural influences shaping the main idea or conflict.

Examine the thematic thread connecting the following summative performance assessment tasks. As students complete each task in the course of a unit of instruction, they pick up information and ideas that will help with the next task. Integrating the summative performance tasks allows for natural reinforcement and extension of the unit's concepts. The continuity helps the teacher and the students stay focused. Students benefit by adding to their learning through the assessment and thus are better prepared for the next task.

Integrated Performance Assessment Tasks [17]			
Level	**Interpretive**	**Presentational**	**Interpersonal**
Novice Theme: Who am I? Who are you?	Watch a video of three students introducing themselves (videotaped exchange students); on a grid of topics that would logically be part of such an introduction, identify the topics actually mentioned and list any details understood on a topic.	Write a description of yourself accompanied by photos. The description will serve as a letter of introduction to a host family where you will be staying on a school trip abroad.	To prepare for the first night at a host family's home, pair up and practice what you might say and what you might be asked by the host family; introduce yourself by sharing the letter and photos prepared as the presentational assessment; ask questions about each other's likes and dislikes.
Intermediate-Low	**Interpretive**	**Presentational**	**Interpersonal**
Theme: Cultural Celebrations	Read information from a website about a specific cultural event in the target country. To gauge comprehension, describe details understood under the categories given by the teacher.	Prepare an entry to put in the website's "Guest Book" including brief biographical data and a reaction to the website, making a comparison to similar cultural events in your own country.	Discuss with a partner the information learned about the cultural event and your own insights about what is similar and different compared to your own family experiences.
Intermediate-Mid	**Interpretive**	**Interpersonal**	**Presentational**
Theme: Fame	Read magazine articles about well-known persons from the target culture; write a summary of the article highlighting the most important information about the person. State why the person is significant in the target culture and if that fame would translate internationally (and to the United States).	In small groups, discuss what makes a person famous. Include the advantages and disadvantages of being famous. Include a personal opinion about the desirability of being famous some day.	Write an essay about fame. Give examples of people from the target culture who are famous and why they are famous. Note the difference between being famous within a country and being famous on an international level. Discuss the positive and negative aspects of fame.
Pre-Advanced	**Presentational**	**Interpretive**	**Interpersonal**
Theme: Cultural Perspectives	Prepare a five-minute speech on a cultural celebration embedded in the target culture, contrasting and comparing the cultural practices and attitudes between a similar demographic group in the United States and in the target culture.	Listen to three classmates' presentations. Summarize the key points made in their presentations. Contrast the perspective of each speaker with your personal perspective gained in your preparation for the presentational component.	Try to picture yourself in the target country during this cultural celebration. Share what you think your personal reaction would be and explain why. Clarify how your perspective is the same or different compared to the one that is commonly held in the target culture. Compare your perspective to the one held by your conversation partner.

DOING IT ON YOUR OWN

Step Five: Fine-Tune and Integrate the Summative Performance Tasks

Thematic focus (from Step One):

(Example: What makes a good friend? How am I a good friend to others?)

Targeted language level, functions emphasized in this unit (verified through Step Three):

(Example: Novice–Describe with lists of adjectives or verbs)

Evaluate what students will do in each of the three summative performance tasks (Step Five)

Write down the three tasks you have identified as the end-of-unit summative assessments for each mode of communication: interpretive, interpersonal, and presentational.

Ask: Will these summative tasks elicit the language I have targeted?

As a result of your evaluation, adapt the tasks to better elicit the targeted language.

As a result of your evaluation, decide the order of the performance assessment tasks, creating a logical link of one task to the next.

Step Six: Incorporate Other Standards to Enrich the Unit of Instruction and Performance Tasks

Up to this point, the focus has been on the development of student language proficiency. The national standards (and most state standards) for learning languages incorporate "the 5 Cs": communication, cultures, connections, comparisons, and communities. In instruction and assessment, these 5 Cs are not equal; they are not each 20% of class time or 20% of a grade. As shown in Figure 3, the central focus is on the three modes of communication, but communication always takes place embedded in culture. Culture is not to be ignored, but it has a different relationship to the evaluation involved in a performance assessment task. Culture may be part of the evaluation in a performance assessment, such as the appropriate use of greetings and other gestures, the use of the culturally accurate format in a letter or a speech, or attention to cultural connotations of words or perspectives. Culture may be built into the evaluation tools, possibly through the assessment task rubric, through a specific presentational assessment task, or through a portfolio reflection where students document their change over time.

The other 3 Cs (connections, comparisons, and communities) likewise play a different role in a performance assessment task. These three goals provide a sense of application and broadened context, but they are not at the heart of assessment. Connections, comparisons, and communities serve as reminders to use the unit and its assessments to guide students to acquire perspectives in other disciplines, deepen understanding of language and culture, and apply language skills at home and abroad, either virtually or face-to-face. This enriches the unit, but is not at the center of the feedback or accountability built into the performance assessments. These goals enrich the unit, but they are not the focus of the performance assessment.

In content-based instruction, content and language are the goals. Likewise in immersion programs, the goals of the connected subject area are intertwined completely with the goals of learning to use the language. For example, early elementary grade programs commonly integrate social studies, language arts, and the world language. Whether in Chinese, German, or Spanish, students might explore the questions: "Where do we live? How is our home community the same or different from a community found in a country where the language being studied is spoken?" Through applications of the language, practice of language arts, and practice of social studies skills, students demonstrate growth in both language and non-language objectives. Such programs incorporate an additional element with the language content.

In Step Six, the teacher enriches the unit of instruction and the performance tasks by checking on ways to incorporate other standards (culture, connections, comparisons, and communities). See Appendix E for examples of ways to include elements of culture in performance assessment tasks.

Figure 3. Standards-Based Performance Assessment[18]

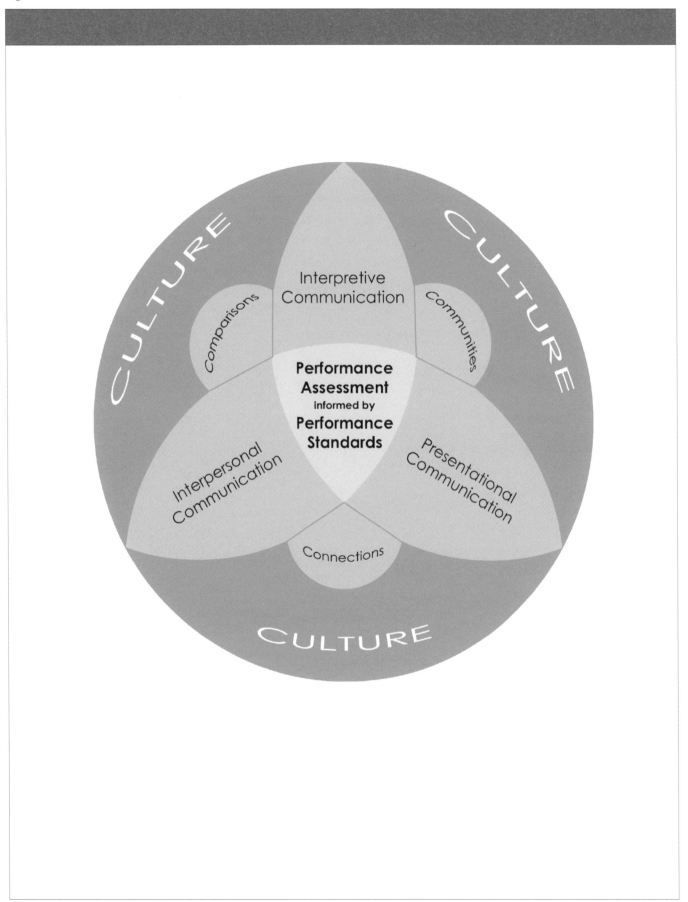

DOING IT ON YOUR OWN

Step Six: Incorporate Other Standards to Enrich the Unit of Instruction and Performance Tasks

Thematic focus (from Step One):

(Example: What makes a good friend? How am I a good friend to others?)

Incorporate other standards to enrich the unit of instruction and performance tasks (Step Six)

What elements of culture might enrich this unit (content knowledge or functional skills)?

What elements of other disciplines (connections) might enrich this unit?

What understandings of languages and cultures might enrich this unit?

What applications in multilingual communities at home or abroad might enrich this unit?

Step Seven: Pilot with Students and Use the Results to Adjust the Assessment Tasks

Trying this out with your students will provide the reality check that is critical for success. Students will ask all the tough questions about the performance assessment tasks, wanting to know logistical details about the performance expected: how, how much, how long, how many, and so on.

Approach your first attempts to use performance assessment tasks as an opportunity to hone your skill at writing and administering them. You will learn from the results.

DOING IT ON YOUR OWN

Step Seven: Pilot with Real Students and Use the Results to Adjust the Assessment Tasks

Thematic focus (from Step One):

(Example: What makes a good friend? How am I a good friend to others?)

Plan to pilot the performance assessment tasks with real students (Step Seven)

Decide if you will use only some students to pilot the tasks, one class, or one level.

Identify how you will use the results in the "pilot" phase.

Will students be held accountable? Will it be part of a unit's assessments?

Will the results become part of their grade (or be used to verify existing grades)?

Use the results to adjust the assessment tasks (Step Seven)

Examine the language samples elicited: Did the tasks elicit the performance desired?

Did the feedback mechanism provide focused information to help improve student performance?

Template

Quick Summary

Reproduce this template to develop future performance assessment tasks for your units of instruction.

What Is the Target for Performance?

Think about the unit you are planning: What is the engaging thematic focus?

What are the assessment targets for interpretive, interpersonal, and presentational communication? Do these assessments engage and motivate your students?

Interpretive Performance	Interpersonal Performance	Presentational Performance

Activities to Prepare for These Performance Assessments

Interpretive Practice	Interpersonal Practice	Presentational Practice

Knowledge Students Need to Be Successful on These Performance Assessments

Language Functions	Vocabulary	Structures

Chapter 4: Designing Rubrics to Assess Performance

Step-by-Step Process for Designing Rubrics

1. Identify what makes a quality performance

2. Evaluate the qualities against the characteristics of the targeted level of proficiency

3. Describe the performance that meets your expectations with the specificity and clarity that will focus your instruction and student learning

4. Describe the performance that exceeds your expectations and the performance that does not meet your expectations

5. Pilot with students and revise based on student work and feedback

6. Determine how you will communicate the assessment results (including using rubrics in grades and incorporating feedback into your instruction)

When asked how their child did in a game, at a concert, in an art project, or in summer reading, parents typically respond that their child did great or not so well, describe an area where he or she really improved, point out some specific elements that were outstanding or at least better than last time, identify some aspects of the performance that he or she should work on, and end with another general comment. It is easy to imagine this conversation because it feels natural and it is how we would expect a performance to be evaluated. The parents focus on an overall evaluation of what they saw and instantly compare their child's performance to how the child did the last time and also how the child is doing in comparison with peers. The emphasis is on feedback to guide improvement, while encouraging their child to keep at it.

This conversation does not focus on an abstract score or grade, but is all about the performance. Coaching to improve performance does not rely on a score or number. Improvement of the child's performance occurs when the parents consider generally agreed-upon criteria and provide feedback to help the child improve by more closely demonstrating those criteria in future performances. How closely do language classrooms replicate this coaching style of evaluation? This chapter provides a step-by-step approach to providing feedback aimed at improving student performance using language in tasks that mirror applications in the real world.

Three terms are often used interchangeably: assessment, evaluation, and grading. The differences can be explained with great clarity as follows: Think of assessment as the means through which student performances will be elicited; evaluation as the process by which teachers judge the excellence of that performance; and grading as the more mechanical compilation of various elements in certain percentages to generate a single rating meant to summarize achievement over a period of time (quarter or semester).[1]

What Insights on Designing Rubrics Are Implied from Research?

Focused Feedback is Critical to Help Learning:

- Vygotsky (1978) identifies the Zone of Proximal Development where learners move from their "actual development level" to a "potential development level" by interaction with others (adults or stronger peers), exceeding what the learner can do alone.

- Shrum and Glisan (2005) conclude that teachers can effectively provide assistance to help a learner move to the potential development level by encouraging motivation, providing focused feedback, modeling, and reducing frustration.

Definitions of Communicative Competence Provide Criteria for Rubrics:

- Shrum and Glisan (2005) summarize research on communicative competence, defining it as "the ability to function in a communicative setting by using not only grammatical knowledge but also gestures and intonation, strategies for making oneself understood, and risk-taking in attempting communication (Bachman, 1990; Campbell and Wales, 1970; Canale and Swain, 1980; Hymes, 1972; Savignon, 1972)." (p. 13)

- Celce-Murcia, Dörnyei, and Thurrell (1995) define communicative competence as discourse competence (language elements or words and phrases) supported by sociocultural competence (stylistic appropriateness, nonverbal expression, and cultural knowledge), linguistic competence (syntax, vocabulary, morphology), and actional competence (matching form to intent) sustained by strategic competence (compensating for deficiencies in the other competencies).

Characteristics of Effective Communication Generate Criteria Useful for Rubric Development:

- Bacon (1992) identifies specific characteristics of successful listeners that include a reluctance to use English when other strategies are not working, the ability to summarize and add details, the ability to use personal knowledge or knowledge of the world or of discourse, not distracted by unknown vocabulary, comfortable hypothesizing and then realistically evaluating alternative interpretations.

- Doughty and Pica (1986) and Porter (1986) show that when pair work involves discussion and negotiation of meaning, students use more content clarifications and comprehension checks.

- Shrum and Glisan (2005) summarize research on error correction and feedback:
  - Feedback should focus on understanding the message, not just on accuracy of form.
  - Feedback should provide comments to help the students' focus on negotiation of meaning.

- Frantzen (1995) finds that explicit grammar instruction has little to no effect on grammatical accuracy in presentational writing.

- Coombs (1986) concludes that skill in using language structures in communication develops outside of knowledge and use of grammar.

- Cohen (1987) and Cohen and Cavalcanti (1990) find that teachers' comments on writing are not usually useful due to being too short and not informative.

- Semke (1984) finds that students make more progress in language ability and writing when teacher feedback consists of comments as opposed to corrections.

- Shrum & Glisan (2005) summarize Ferris (2003) as suggesting "that teachers should recognize that, at the lower levels of proficiency, feedback should be targeted and brief, focusing on a couple of points, whether related to content or form, at a time." (p. 300)

To measure student improvement in proficiency when using the target language, assessment is setting up the tasks that will get students to produce a sample of language. The goal is to generate a language sample that is sufficient in length and content to be evaluated. The parameters of the task need to be arranged both to motivate students to perform their best and to pull out the type of language skills and characteristics that will match selected criteria.

Evaluation must be based on consistent and appropriate criteria. Often an unintended consequence of the evaluation tool is that students receive skewed ratings based on elements that are not really part of language proficiency. When rubrics reward quantity (e.g., five sentences or questions, 10 past-tense verbs, three paragraphs) or non-language elements (e.g., use of color on a cover, inclusion of three quotes or four references), the student does not receive guidance on how to improve the language performance. Educators must carefully craft or select their evaluation instruments to ensure that they are measuring what really matters.

Grading is often subject to local policies, either district- or school-level. Grades in themselves do not help students identify the strengths and weaknesses of their performance in order to improve. In the author's experience, the typical reaction when students get back quizzes, tests, or projects with a letter or number grade attached is not an analysis or reflection in order to improve. Unfortunately, all the work that went into grading produced little reflection on the part of the students as to the strength or weakness of their performance. Students seemed to believe that grading is a process of accumulating enough points to get a certain grade for the term, not an integral part of learning and improving.

Rubrics to Improve Performance

This chapter focuses on effective evaluation: providing feedback based on criteria to improve performance. The key mechanism for that feedback is a rubric designed to describe the expectations for performance. A rubric is a set of criteria by which student work is evaluated. Rubrics are usually arranged in a table format showing at least three levels of quality: exceeding expectations, meeting expectations, and not meeting expectations. The three levels of quality are described for each of the criteria identified as important to the performance. A well-crafted rubric describes the expected performance in words that are clear to students.

When Are Rubrics an Effective Feedback Tool?

Not all the time! Consider various types of assessments. When is it worth your time to develop and use rubrics?

Sometimes teachers are only looking for information on how well students can use a new grammatical structure or how well they have learned vocabulary. A performance task is not needed to find out this information. A simple worksheet or quiz will more efficiently provide the information the teacher needs and do so in a more timely manner. Performance tasks take time to administer and to evaluate. Sometimes, quick learning checks are needed and a true–false exercise, multiple-choice items, or brief quiz may be more efficient for obtaining the specific information needed at a particular point in time. Worksheets provide feedback on how well students can manipulate a particular verb form. A rough draft provides information on how well students have organized their thoughts and creatively expressed them. Sometimes a simple yes/no check activity is all that is needed. At times, a fast rating of "no response," "adequate response," or "exceptional response" may be exactly what will provide a check on specific learning. An important gauge is to match the feedback tool to the type of assessment. Formative assessments, being simpler, shorter, and more limited in scope, may not necessarily require a rubric. Summative assessments elicit a more complex performance from students and therefore warrant the time needed to develop a rubric that can provide extensive feedback.

In addition, the choice of feedback needs to match the language level. At the Novice-Low or Novice-Mid-levels, there is not a lot to distinguish a student's performance other than identifying whether the student accomplished the task or not. At the Novice-Low and Novice-Mid-levels, language is so memorized and predictable that it becomes difficult to describe much more in a rubric than the simple accomplishment of the task.

Teachers will want to use a rubric to help students know what is expected on a summative assessment. Students need to understand the various elements in a rubric which will be used at the end of a unit. During the unit, when students practice evaluating each other on single elements of the rubric, they build understanding of what counts. Teachers might pull one criterion and use it both as a focus for instruction and as a focus for feedback on pair activities and other tasks. Students might also view a performance together and analyze it based on a single criterion, again in order to develop a common understanding of that element of the rubric. Then, when the rubric is used for a summative assessment, students will not be surprised. They will benefit from familiarity with the rubric and its criteria.

Later, in Chapter 5, readers will be introduced to techniques for engaging students in the development of rubrics. Again, the goal is to help students become familiar with those elements that are critical for improving language proficiency.

Real-World Example—Evaluating a Presenter

Imagine that as a workshop begins you are asked to evaluate the presenter. You are not provided with a form to fill in, so you have to develop your own criteria.

Step One: Your first step is to decide: *What makes for a quality performance?* You draw on much prior experience as a workshop participant in order to answer that question.

What criteria might come to mind?
- Hooks the audience
- Keeps it interesting
- Tells real stories, convinces with good evidence
- Sticks to the topic
- Uses images to hold and focus interest
- Looks at the audience
- Does not read a script

Step Two: Your second step is to *evaluate the qualities against the characteristics of the targeted level of proficiency.* Your expectations need to reflect the presenter's prior experience.

You naturally want to compare your criteria for a quality performance to what is reasonable to expect based on the presenter's background and experience. If the presenter is well-known with many years of experience and success, expectations are higher for the "proficiency" level of the performance. On the other hand, if this is the first workshop ever given by this presenter, the participants will be more forgiving on some criteria and might select other characteristics as more appropriate for first-time presenters.

Keeping in mind differing levels of experience or "proficiency," you might sort out the criteria something like the following chart.

First-Time Presenter	Experienced Presenter
• Looks at the audience • Does not read a script • Sticks to the topic • Shares personal examples	• Hooks the audience • Keeps it interesting • Uses images to hold and focus interest • Tells real stories, convinces with good evidence

The important lesson is to match the characteristics to a realistic expectation based on the level of proficiency of the performer.

Step Three: Your next step is to *describe the performance that meets your expectations with specificity and clarity* so you can provide helpful feedback to the presenter.

In order to do this, you need to pull the ideas into manageable categories. You have created a rather random list of many items. You realize that many of your descriptors of a great presenter cluster together around a few larger categories.

You group the descriptors as follows:
1. Sticks to the topic, tells real stories, convinces with good evidence
2. Looks at the audience, does not read a script
3. Shares personal examples, hooks the audience, keeps it interesting, uses images to hold and focus interest

You decide to label these three as content, delivery, and impact. These three categories will work for both first-time presenters and very experienced presenters. As you think about it further, you identify more descriptors for each of your three categories, thinking of what would describe the category at both the beginning and more advanced levels of a presenter.

Category	Descriptors of Performance	Real World Presenter
Content	Fulfills the task Stays on topic Provides accurate information Organizes the information effectively	Tells real stories, convinces with good evidence Sticks to the topic
Speaker's Delivery	Engages the audience Uses appropriate volume and voice quality, varied for effect Uses pacing and processing time effectively	Looks at the audience Does not read a script
Impact	Uses visuals or technology to reinforce message Personalizes examples and the message Engages the audience interactively	Keeps audience's interest with images Hooks the audience Keeps it interesting Shares personal examples

You identify very clearly the performance that will meet your expectations.

Step Four: To help the presenter improve, you next describe the performance that exceeds your expectations and the performance that does not meet your expectations.

Rather than merely saying that the presenter did or did not meet your expectations, you want to provide more specific and useful feedback. By clearly identifying what a performance would look like to exceed your expectations, you are helping the presenter reach for improvement. Also, by describing the performance that does not meet your expectations, you can show specific evidence as to the actions or qualities that were not effective, pointing the way to improvement.

Step Five: Before using your criteria to rate the presenter, you want to pilot with a variety of different presenters and revise based on how the rubric works with real performances and how effective the feedback is in conveying your ideas to the presenter. You want to make sure that the criteria and descriptors are clear and easy to use in evaluating the performance.

Step Six: Finally, you determine how you will communicate the results of your evaluation. Will you just show your rubric and ratings to the presenter? Will you have a post-performance conversation to go over the evidence that led to your ratings? Will your evaluation become the basis for charting improvement from presentation to presentation? The presenter is as much an owner and user of the evaluation as you are.

You are now satisfied that you did not just tell the presenter something meaningless like, "Good job," or "I liked your presentation," or "You kind of lost me." You know that the presenter will be able to focus on what worked and what did not. You look forward to the next time you can see this presenter in action, knowing that the "performance" will be even better because the presenter learned a lot from your feedback through such a carefully designed rubric.

Let's remember the process that was used to develop the rubric for a presenter as we go through the same six steps to design effective rubrics for use in language classrooms.

Step One: Identify What Makes a Quality Performance

In providing feedback, the criteria must be appropriate to the task. What really matters for effective communication? By examining the purpose behind what students are asked to do in the assessment tasks, the teacher can better identify the appropriate criteria. The teacher must consider the mode of communication: interpersonal, interpretive, or presentational. The criteria need to be generated by what makes for effective communication in the specific mode of communication.

Rather than treating all speaking as the same skill, or trying to use the same measures and evaluation criteria for all speaking tasks, consider how speaking for an interpersonal purpose (e.g., agreeing on when to meet) has very different requirements or expectations from speaking for a presentational purpose (e.g., telling classmates about a recent trip). For an interpersonal purpose, critical elements in the evaluation include how well students maintain and sustain the conversation, ask for clarification, and negotiate meaning. The criteria for evaluating a presentational task would include language accuracy, organization of the presentation, appropriateness for the targeted audience, and the impact on that audience. The instrument used for evaluation needs to fit the communicative purpose. Rubrics need to be developed based on the requirements of the communicative task.

When identifying what makes a quality performance for students, consider the performances that you have experienced in the past. Use real samples of student work to identify what makes a quality performance. Focus on the characteristics of use of language and try not to be influenced by factors such as neatness or use of color in presentational tasks, humor in interpersonal tasks, and over-reliance on specific details in interpretive tasks. These factors are not essential to the language performance and may distract from what really counts.

What counts? It depends on the mode of communication. To identify what makes a quality performance, consider these general differences by mode of communication, regardless of level of language proficiency.

Interpretive:

- Level of detail understood
- Ability to provide a summary
- Able to use context clues to help comprehension

Interpersonal:

- Negotiation of meaning
- Use of strategies when there is lack of comprehension
- Means of asking for clarification
- Ability to sustain a conversation

Presentational:

- Accuracy of vocabulary and structure
- Organization and flow

- Impact on the audience
- Use of clear and supportive examples

These are big, broad categories. The idea is to begin to frame the characteristics on which the rubric will be built. This is still a brainstorming phase, beginning to narrow from all that is possible to use as criteria for the rubric and starting to focus on those elements that are most important for this task, at this stage of language development, and at this point in the school year. It is natural to try to put into a rubric everything that could possibly be evaluated in a given performance. However, putting too many elements into the rubric will only make it difficult for the teacher to administer and will reduce its meaningfulness to students. Both teachers and students should concentrate on just a few key criteria during any given performance, rather than trying to juggle an overwhelming number of elements. Over time, different rubrics will address all of the critical criteria. Eventually, students will receive feedback on all the criteria; they just do not need to think about all of them at once.

Idea of Non-Negotiables[2]

Often a teacher will see a performance that feels like it is exactly what she has been trying to develop in her students, but the student does not do well on the rubric and scores lower than the teacher felt the performance warranted. Likewise, at times, a student produces a performance that is too predictable and safe or too limited in showing growth in language proficiency, and yet the rubric delivers a score that rewards the performance at a much higher level than the teacher felt the performance deserved. The issue is usually that the rubric focused on the wrong criteria. Rather than identifying what makes a quality performance, the rubric probably listed other criteria that did not really contribute to a quality performance. The teacher needs to ask what is being measured. The message the teacher wants students to internalize is that just looking good or playing it safe is not going to lead to improved proficiency. The criteria need to support that message by focusing on what really counts to improve language proficiency.

Think about the messages students receive from the rubric on the next page.

Interpersonal Conversation–Intermediate Level

Does Not Meet Expectations	Meets Expectations	Exceeds Expectations
Asks a few questions	Asks five questions	Asks more than five questions
Words	Phrases	Complete sentences
Dull	Interesting	Energetic
Less than 1 minute	1 to 1.5 minutes	At least 2 minutes

The message given to students is that they need to count how many questions they ask, they should use complete sentences, and the goal is really to fill two minutes. What they will ask is, what do "interesting" and "energetic" look like? Yes, the intention is to bring more engagement to the task and to have students show that they are able to use Intermediate-level language, which is characterized as at the sentence level, but the real result is that students will pay attention to elements that signal higher levels of proficiency but will not focus on communication at all. The number of questions should be based on a task that requires students to negotiate meaning, so they focus on their communication rather than on just counting the questions. The focus on the number of questions allows students to argue that simply saying "Why?" should count as a question and the rubric criteria would allow them to repeat the same question five times. Students will think about asking their questions and will not really care what the other person says in reply, since nothing on the rubric addresses comprehension. This is not the intended result! The non-negotiables should be that students have to talk for at least two minutes and that they have to both ask and answer questions. This allows the teacher to focus on the quality of language. Once a language sample that meets these non-negotiables is obtained, the teacher can focus on the quality of language in the rubric and not on requirements that simply generate a sample of appropriate length and content.

The same is true in the presentational mode. Below is a project rubric that is trying to make sure that students do everything they are supposed to in order to create a quality product.

Travel Brochure Project–Intermediate Level

Criteria	Does Not Meet Expectations	Meets Expectations	Exceeds Expectations
Amount of descriptive language used	Words	Phrases	Sentences
Accuracy	Spelling errors and grammatical mistakes	Spelling errors and correct grammar	Correct spelling and correct grammar
Accuracy and amount of factual information	3	5	7
Resources	Book only	At least one outside source	At least two sources, including "real people"
Material used	Pencil and notebook paper	Unlined paper; black and white	Unlined paper, neat with color
Illustration	None	Black and white	Color

Again, the messages given to students are not about the quality of the language produced. Non-negotiables in the rubric divert student focus from language to production values. If the teacher wants students to use two sources of information, to interview at least one person, to prepare the travel brochure on unlined paper, and to include color illustrations, then this becomes the assignment. Once the assignment is complete, once the non-negotiables have been met, now the student is ready to present the quality product that is worth the teacher's time to evaluate on a rubric that will provide feedback on the quality of the language performance. In the presentational mode, other examples of non-negotiables to help prepare a quality performance are the note cards prepared for an oral presentation or the rough draft that precedes the final essay. The items that go into preparing for the performance task should not be part of the evaluative rubric. Instead, those items that are only quantity and not quality may count as homework or in-class participation credit.

The message of quality should also be realistic. In this presentational example, it is unreasonable to expect Intermediate students to have perfectly correct spelling or grammar in an on-demand situation. It may be reasonable to expect students to produce sentence-level language; however, aren't actual travel brochures often filled with words and phrases to catch the reader's attention? The teacher likely has other evidence of a student's ability to use full sentences. The strategies that make an effective brochure are what should be encouraged through the rubric. A quality performance should reflect what is possible for students at their level of development of language proficiency as well as what is effective and important in real-life applications of the same task.

The list of criteria in a rubric should contain the elements that you want students to think about during the performance. Choose wisely!

In the interpretive performance, what should be the focus for students during their investigation or search for meaning? Should it be on translating every word? Should students be thinking about memorizing the facts in preparation for a multiple-choice check at the end of the reading? The feedback instead should focus on how much detail students are able to pull out of what they are reading, hearing, or viewing in the target language; the variety of strategies students use to understand when vocabulary or structures are not known; or how well students can identify the main idea and the author's point or perspective.

In the interpersonal performance, what should be on students' minds as they spontaneously work through an exchange of information? Is it the number of questions they need to ask? Is it their use of a particular verb form (e.g., use subjunctive six times)? Or, instead, should students be thinking about working with their conversation partner to come to the conclusion targeted by the task? We want students focusing on working with their partner to figure out what each other is expressing. Students should be trying to maintain the conversation by asking great follow-up questions and providing their own examples.

In the presentational performance, what should students be thinking about as they deliver a well-planned or well-rehearsed presentation, either written or spoken? What will count? Is it the original outline or the color on the cover? If these elements have already been evaluated as check-in assignments, students do not need to be checked on these elements again as part of the rubric evaluating the performance. Is feedback only focused on the grammatical accuracy and complex sentence structure? Teachers should ask themselves: What makes writing powerful? Real-life examples will allow teachers to identify the criteria that actually will lead to powerful expression, either written, spoken, or visually represented. Capturing and maintaining the audience's attention; guiding the reader, listener, or viewer with logical organization and clear expression; and personalizing the presentation with illustrative examples are all critical elements that result in a powerful presentation. It is not that accuracy does not matter; it is that accuracy is only one element and it must not dominate the other elements needed to be effective in the presentational mode.

The important lesson is to remove what does not matter in describing a quality performance. In addition, remove the non-negotiables; that is, those elements that must be present in order to have a performance worth taking the time to evaluate using the rubric. See p. 44 for an example of identifying elements of a quality performance.

DOING IT ON YOUR OWN

Step One: Identify What Makes a Quality Performance

Thematic focus:

(Example: What makes a good friend? How am I a good friend to others?)

Vocabulary and grammar focus:

(Example: Adjectives of characteristics, verbs in first- and third-person singular)

Targeted language level, functions emphasized in this unit:

(Example: Novice–Describe with lists of adjectives or verbs)

Identify what makes a quality performance (Step One):

(Examples):

- *Uses various strategies when lacking comprehension*
- *Uses strategies to negotiate meaning*
- *Uses effective organization*

Look carefully at the performance tasks you developed for your unit of instruction.

The characteristics of the performance desired will come directly from what students are asked to do. If the interpersonal task does not require any narration or extended description, then that should not be a criterion for evaluation, since you won't see any. If you want students to show some ability to narrate or tell a story, make sure the task requires students to use that skill.

List the qualities you want to see in the specific performance for the mode of communication being assessed.

Interpretive	*Interpersonal*	*Presentational*

Travel Unit Example–Intermediate Level

Why would I choose a particular destination?		
Interpretive	**Presentational**	**Interpersonal**
Using Internet resources, fill in requested information about the area you have selected to visit in the target country.	Create a commercial and a flyer to promote the region you have selected.	Discuss with a partner the places in classmates' commercials, deciding which will be the most exciting to visit and how you will convince the rest of your class.
What makes a quality performance?		
• Uses skim and scan techniques to find appropriate details • Can summarize, not just copy, the key details	• Catches and maintains attention of audience • Provides accurate details • Convinces by providing multiple reasons to visit the region	• Asks for information and provides own responses • Asks for clarification when there is lack of comprehension • Encourages partner to continue the conversation (takes responsibility for keeping it going)

Step Two: Evaluate the Qualities Against the Characteristics of the Targeted Level of Proficiency

In the example presented earlier in this chapter, the participants at a workshop or conference session should probably take into consideration the level of expertise and experience of a presenter before judging the presenter's performance. A colleague presenting for the first time will likely be judged with more empathy than a well-known speaker. Likewise, students at the beginning of their language learning need to be evaluated on criteria that match their level of proficiency. The qualities should provide a holistic appraisal of their use of language, but through the lens of empathy for their attempts to communicate. The rubric should validate these attempts.

Consider how native speakers evaluate student performance. A U.S. teacher shared the story of using visiting educators from France to help administer interpersonal assessments to her students.[3] The visiting native speakers sat and talked with students one-on-one about topics drawn from the semester's units. The teacher then asked the visiting teachers to characterize how well each student could communicate in the interpersonal mode. Their evaluation report surprised the U.S. teacher because it only focused on how well students were able to maintain the conversation by sharing stories, telling their personal experiences, and asking questions of the visitors. No mention was made of grammatical errors or limited vocabulary. When asked why they did not bring up accuracy of grammar or vocabulary, the visitors said that they were fo-

cused on the exchange of ideas and the message of the student. They said that they did not even think about the grammar or vocabulary, because if there was a lack of comprehension, they and the student asked questions back and forth, working out the failure to communicate until comprehension was restored. The native speakers focused on the message and not on how it was being conveyed.

Another teacher tells of how she wanted to provide her elementary students of Spanish with a more authentic assessment.[4] She was fortunate to be able to work with native-speaking parents of some of the students. She had parents come in to chat with her students on topics that came directly from recent units of instruction, such as their neighborhood, their school, and their families. Seeking an overall rating of her students, the teacher asked of the parents only that they rate each student as "really good at communicating," "able to communicate with only some occasional difficulty," or "often having difficulty communicating." The parents reported that almost all the students were really good at communicating. The teacher was surprised and asked the parents about the language the students were using. The parents said that they were impressed with the confidence displayed by the students and their ability to use their limited language skills to really engage in a conversation by asking questions and providing information.

When developing rubrics, teachers must strive to adopt the attitude of these native speakers in order to realistically evaluate student performance with regard to the targeted level of proficiency. The attitude should be that the beginning students are pretty good for beginners, not that they are lousy as native speakers. Educators should match their expectations to the targeted level of proficiency as they evaluate students. A deficit model that counts errors does not realistically reflect what can be expected at the Novice, Intermediate, and even Advanced levels, where perfection does not occur in spontaneous performances. The grammar and vocabulary can be more isolated in formative assessments, but in the summative assessments, they become only means to an end, with the real focus being on the strength of communication. Appendix F links proficiency levels to the expectations in real-world jobs.

Very broadly, the *ACTFL Performance Guidelines for K–12 Learners* present proficiency targets that help set realistic expectations against which to evaluate what makes a quality performance at each level: Novice, Intermediate, and Pre-Advanced. The descriptions are rich in detail. The value of the performance guidelines is that they are matched to the mode of communication being used in the performance task: interpretive, interpersonal, and presentational.

The categories of the *ACTFL Performance Guidelines for K–12 Learners* are:

- *Comprehensibility*
  How well is the student understood?
  (interpersonal and presentational modes only)
- *Comprehension*
  How well does the student understand?
  (interpersonal and interpretive modes only)
- *Language Control*
  How accurate is the student's language?
- *Vocabulary*
  How extensive and applicable is the student's vocabulary?
- *Cultural Awareness*
  How is the student's cultural knowledge reflected in language use?
- *Communication Strategies*
  How does the student maintain communication?

Language teachers at a workshop[5] summarized the details for each category as follows:

	Comprehensibility	Comprehension	Language Control	Vocabulary	Cultural Awareness	Communication Strategies
Novice	Predictable; Rehearsed; Imitation; Rely on more than just verbal cues	Gestures; Gist; Cognates; Familiar topics	Accurate with memorized material; Fall back on formulas; Inaccurate when trying to create	Everyday words; Pantomime; Occasionally use native language; Memorized; Limited in number (lots of cognates used)	Imitate; Recognize similarities; Use native culture except if memorized target culture (e.g., gestures)	Visual clues; Repetition; Previous (background) knowledge
Intermediate	Express own thoughts; Recognize patterns; Understood by teacher and peers	Branch out from known to unknown; Longer and more complex; Contextual clues	More inferences; Can get meaning from the unfamiliar; Put sentences together	More daring and open to experimentation (mistakes); Aware of sentence structure; Use affirmative/ negative and context clues	Recognize differences; Make comparisons	Expansion; Circumlocute; Inferences
Pre-Advanced	Control of tenses; Continuity with fewer pauses; Detailed /depth of expressions	Details with inferences; Cultural nuances; Can clarify and transfer to another context	Capable of complexity; Still present-tense-bound; More idiomatic usage	Culturally authentic expressions; Variety and use of idioms; Use target language to define target language	Analyze perspectives; Use appropriate gestures; Use idioms	Sustain use of target language; Degree of analysis/ depth; Refining and detailed

Travel Unit Example–Intermediate Level

Why would I choose a particular destination?		
Interpretive	**Presentational**	**Interpersonal**
Using Internet resources, fill in requested information about the area you have selected to visit in the target country.	Create a commercial and a flyer to promote the region you have selected.	Discuss with a partner the places in classmates' commercials, deciding which will be the most exciting to visit and how you will convince the rest of your class.
• Uses skim and scan techniques to find appropriate details • Can summarize, not just copy, the key details	• Catches and maintains attention of audience • Provides accurate details • Convinces by providing multiple reasons to visit the region	• Asks for information and provides own responses • Asks for clarification when there is lack of comprehension • Encourages partner to continue the conversation (takes responsibility for keeping it going)
Step Two: Refined in comparison with Intermediate-level performance guidelines		
• Pulls appropriate details from Internet resources of varying lengths • Evidence of using context clues and simple inferences to comprehend details • Comprehends more than just the gist [How students accomplish this cannot be controlled, so "uses skim and scan techniques" might occur, but cannot be evaluated in this rubric]	• Sufficient accuracy to be understood by teacher and peers • Uses strategies to maintain audience's attention • Makes the case for visiting the region ["Provides accurate details" becomes a non-negotiable element evaluated in a rough draft; not part of the quality of the language performance to be evaluated in this rubric]	• Expresses own thoughts • Uses circumlocution as necessary • Recombines learned vocabulary and structures in simple sentences • Asks for clarification by repeating words and sometimes selecting substitute words • Uses various strategies to maintain the conversation

Another way to gauge the appropriateness of the selected criteria is to examine the "Can Do" statements of LinguaFolio[6] for the targeted level of proficiency (see Appendix G). Written in student-friendly terms, the LinguaFolio statements capture the expected level of performance through specific observable language behaviors. At Concordia Language Villages in Minnesota, LinguaFolio formed the basis of the CLVisa,[7] in which performance targets were captured in statements that helped villagers understand the expected language performance. See sample "Can Do" statements on p. 48.

DOING IT ON YOUR OWN

Step Two: Evaluate the Qualities Against the Characteristics of the Targeted Level of Proficiency

Thematic focus (from Step One):
(Example: What makes a good friend? How am I a good friend to others?)

Targeted language level, functions emphasized in this unit:
(Example: Novice–Describe with lists of adjectives or verbs)

Mode of communication:
(Interpretive, interpersonal, or presentational)

Match the list of what makes a quality performance, from Step One, to the characteristics of the targeted level of proficiency.

Look again at the chart of language levels and examine the *ACTFL Performance Guidelines for K–12 Learners* to focus on the qualities of performance to expect at the targeted proficiency level (Novice, Intermediate, Pre-Advanced).

Edit the criteria.

As a filter to select or re-phrase the criteria, ask:

1. Is this criterion appropriate for this proficiency level?

2. How might I rephrase this criterion to better match the expectation of this proficiency level?

3. What criteria did I miss that I want to have students think about during this performance task?

Write the revised descriptions of the performance expectation for the mode of communication being assessed, refined by the targeted proficiency level.

Sample "Can Do" Statements from Concordia Language Villages' Explorer [8]

"Can Do" Statements–Interpersonal Mode				
Categories	**Surviving** ——→	**Exploring** ——→	**Engaging** ——→	**Established**
1. Asking and Responding to Questions	I can respond to a simple question, like "What is your name?"	I can ask and respond to simple, memorized questions	I can ask and respond with details to who, what, when, and why questions	I can maintain a conversation, asking and responding to questions and follow-up questions	I can sustain a conversation, asking and responding to detailed questions with follow-ups
2. Expressing Feelings and Emotions	I can say that I am happy, sad	I can express my emotions in simple sentences	I can express emotions such as surprise, happiness, anger and sadness with some explanation	I can express and react to a variety of emotions and feelings giving detailed explanations	I can clearly express my emotions and feelings using precise vocabulary and detailed explanations
3. Expressing Preferences and Opinions	When asked, I can respond with "I like/ don't like it"	I can ask and respond to questions about my likes and dislikes	I can share with someone my personal preferences and opinions with simple reasons	I can share with someone my personal preferences and opinions, offering detailed explanations to support my opinions	I can provide a detailed rationale or argument to support my opinion on a wide variety of topics
4. Telling or Retelling Stories	I can say what I am doing in short, memorized sentences	I can tell someone about my day in short, simple sentences	I can tell a story in a series of sentences	I can tell about something that happened or will happen giving the sequence of events	I can tell a detailed story using paragraph-length narration to describe the event
5. Carrying on a Conversation	I can exchange greetings/farewells	I can participate in a short conversation on very familiar topics	I can carry on a conversation on a variety of topics that are familiar to me	I can initiate and maintain a conversation with ease and confidence on a variety of topics	I can sustain a conversation on a wide variety of topics and appropriately handled an unexpected event or complication
6. Describing People, Places, Things	I can describe using one or two words	I can describe using short sentences	I can describe using many adjectives	I can use a variety of descriptors in several long sentences	I can give precise and detailed descriptions of paragraph length

Step Three: Describe the Performance That Meets Your Expectations with the Specificity and Clarity That Will Focus Your Instruction and Student Learning

You enter Step Three with clear criteria that describe a quality performance, checked for appropriateness at the targeted level of proficiency. Now you turn to how to present the criteria in terms that will be clear to students while also focusing them on what they need to work on to improve their performance.

At this point, you need to decide: are you developing a rubric that is holistic or analytic?

There are advantages and disadvantages to both. To decide, consider the purpose for using the rubric. Is it being used as a gauge of how students are performing at the beginning and end

of a long period of time? Choose holistic. Is it being used as a gauge of how students are performing at a unit level? Choose analytic. Will the teacher and students be comfortable with a general rating? Choose holistic. Will the teacher and students benefit from the profile of several different criteria? Choose analytic. Can the feedback be general, more to verify other assessment evidence? Choose holistic. Do teacher and students need specific feedback that can shape goals for improvement? Choose analytic. It is critical to decide how specific the feedback must be in order to be useful to teacher and students. For most unit-level summative assessments, an analytic rubric that identifies both strengths and weaknesses provides the specificity that will help students know what they need to do to improve.

Rubrics take time to develop. One will likely avoid developing rubrics if they are too general and not useful in forming part of the evaluation of students. Later in this chapter, guidance is given on specific strategies for incorporating rubrics into grading. Focus now on how to design an effective rubric for a specific performance assessment task. The categories and descriptors must match the targeted proficiency level, the mode of communication (interpretive, interpersonal, or presentational), and the specific task that students will perform.

As you look at each criterion identified in Step Two, envision the performance that you are expecting to see. What would it sound like? What language would students use? Imagine actual conversations, presentations, and summaries of what was understood. To design effective rubrics, teachers need to think about real language samples. Rubrics must be based on real student performances, not imagined or idealized performances. What can students realistically do? In conversation, it will not be perfect. Students will start and stop, will search for words, will self-correct, will respond with thoughts which are not always complete sentences. In presentational, students will have opportunities to improve and perfect their performance, so the expectation of accuracy is much higher. In the interpretive tasks, it is important to consider how students will demonstrate their interpretation of something read, heard, or viewed. If students must use the target language to explain what they understood in the target language, the teacher will not know if the problem was in the comprehension or in the expression. To isolate the interpretive skill, students may be asked to use their native language (e.g., English), to explain what they understood. This places the evaluation only on comprehension, not complicating the assessment with language production. [Examples of comprehension guides from the IPA project demonstrate this use of English for assessing the interpretive mode of communication. See Appendix C.]

In developing the IPA project, classroom teachers reported that the following criteria seemed best to capture the performance students showed:

Interpretive: Students identified key words of the target language that helped to identify the main idea; students identified in English the key details that explained or supported the main idea; students demonstrated their ability to use context clues to guess the meaning of unknown words and phrases; and Pre-Advanced students were able to make inferences based on the text.

Interpersonal: Students were able to negotiate meaning, students accomplished the given task; communicating the message was more important than accuracy.

Presentational: Organization and impact were hallmarks of performances that met expectations; teachers had a higher expectation of accuracy of structure and vocabulary if students had the opportunity to polish, practice, and rehearse the presentation.

From your list of criteria, then, group together those elements that have a common purpose. In an interpersonal task, repeating what the partner said with a tag to turn it into a question, rephrasing a question, correcting the partner, and using a memorized phrase like "Do you mean to say that … ?" are all examples of asking for clarification. In a presentational task, several items may cluster together around how to maintain the audience's attention. Such grouping makes it possible to focus on a key strategy for success in each mode of communication. As students move to higher levels of proficiency, their repertoire builds and they use more than one approach in any given strategic element of communication. Highlighting the big ideas helps students focus on what will improve their performance before, during, and after the assessment task.

	Holistic	Analytic
Characterized by:	Criteria are combined into a single descriptive paragraph	Criteria are identified and described separately in categories
Useful for:	Broad program checkpoints; Students see if they have performed at the targeted level (or above or below it)	Feedback to focus on specific elements of the performance; Students can see strengths and weaknesses; Provides students with feedback to guide improvement and emphasis (personal goals)
Limited by:	Requires strategic decisions about how to balance various criteria in coming up with the single holistic decision of performance level	Requires strategic decisions as to the weight of various criteria especially if used for a letter grade

Travel Unit Example–Intermediate Level

Why would I choose a particular destination?		
Interpretive	**Presentational**	**Interpersonal**
Using Internet resources, fill in requested information about the area you have selected to visit in the target country.	Create a commercial and a flyer to promote the region you have selected.	Discuss with a partner the places in classmates' commercials, deciding which will be the most exciting to visit and how you will convince the rest of your class.
Step Two: Refined in comparison with Intermediate-level performance guidelines		
• Pulls appropriate details from Internet resources of varying lengths • Evidence of using context clues and simple inferences to comprehend details • Comprehends more than just the gist	• Has sufficient accuracy to be understood by teacher and peers • Uses strategies to maintain audience's attention • Makes the case for visiting the region	• Expresses own thoughts • Uses circumlocution as necessary • Recombines learned vocabulary and structures in simple sentences • Asks for clarification by repeating words and sometimes selecting substitute words • Uses various strategies to maintain the conversation
Step Three: Describe the performance that meets your expectations, with identified categories		
• Main idea: Can identify the main ideas of the various Internet resources • Supporting details: Can identify some supporting details • Inferences: Can use context clues to identify meaning of some new words	• Flow and organization: Provides a logical flow, keeping to main point and providing clear subtopics; uses some cohesive devices to help listener/viewer • Delivery: The message is understood even if errors are present; voice is clear, loud, little hesitation • Maintain audience's attention: Uses visuals to guide the viewer through the presentation	• Communication strategies: Attempts to maintain and sustain the conversation by asking questions and providing personal responses • Asks for clarification: Uses limited strategies, such as repeating words and sometimes selecting substitute words • Comprehensibility: Uses circumlocution when lacking vocabulary; effectively uses words and simple sentences to make ideas known

Step Three: Describe the Performance that Meets Your Expectations with the Specificity and Clarity that Will Focus Your Instruction and Student Learning

Thematic focus:

(Example: What makes a good friend? How am I a good friend to others?)

Targeted language level, functions emphasized in this unit:

(Example: Novice–Describe with lists of adjectives or verbs)

Mode of communication:

(Interpretive, interpersonal, or presentational)

Pull the ideas into logical clusters. By refining your list into manageable categories, you will provide more focus for both instruction and feedback:

(Examples of cluster titles could include):

Interpretive:

Comprehension strategies (Use of context clues, pulling out appropriate inferences)

Depth of detail (Able to identify the gist, the main idea, identifying increasingly sophisticated levels of detail)

continued

continued

Interpersonal:

Maintaining and sustaining the conversation (Using strategies to negotiate meaning)

Asking for clarification

Presentational:

Content

Delivery

Impact

For each cluster, describe exactly what the student performance looks like to **meet** your expectations.

Here are scales of sample criteria from Novice to Pre-Advanced–identified by mode of communication:

These descriptors are designed to help you build your rubric for a specific performance assessment task. For Step Three, locate your "Meets Expectations" on these scales. To help you with Step Three, here are sample categories and descriptors across several "levels" from Novice to Pre-Advanced students. The mode of communication is important to consider as that communicative purpose changes the expectations concerning accuracy and completeness.

Interpretive–Comprehension Strategies

Novice			Intermediate		Pre-Advanced	
Relies on single words, cognates, and graphical evidence (illustrations, titles), visuals, or gestures	Focuses on known words and phrases; some meaning derived from recognizing structural patterns	Some use of hypothesizing to predict what could be in the message; skims and scans to find meaning	Uses context clues to understand new words or phrases (when within student experience)	Uses context clues to understand new words or phrases (based on understanding the gist and less on own experience)	Uses structure or organization (organizing principles) of the text to add to understanding (e.g., pro/con, chronological)	Uses inferences to add to understanding; uses background knowledge of culture or author

Interpretive–Depth of Detail

Novice		Intermediate			Pre-Advanced	
Understanding is limited to the broadest description of the main idea; no accurate identification of supporting ideas	Broad understanding of the main idea; some accurate supporting ideas are included, most are missing or inaccurate	Begins to group supporting ideas into categories to list the key points in support of the main idea	Can synthesize the information into broad categories	Accurately summarizes the main idea and all supporting ideas; any inaccuracies are minor and do not detract from understanding the main idea	Identifies unique perspectives based on the culture or the author's perspective	Accurately adds inferences to expand the main idea and supporting ideas

Interpersonal–Maintaining and Sustaining the Conversation

Novice			Intermediate			Pre-Advanced
Responds when prompted or asked, usually to high-frequency cues; initiation is limited to memorized words or phrases	Mainly in a reactive mode, sticks to direct answers; able to initiate conversation with a few original questions; generally uses yes/no questions	Uses circumlocution to stay in the conversation; maintains conversation with "give and take" vs. turn-taking; uses informational questions (who, what, where, when)	Asks follow-up questions and inserts rejoinders to maintain the conversation and stay on topic	Helps partner by supplying words or finishing sentences or thoughts	Provides own responses to prompt partner (models responses to help partner respond)	Uses transition phrases to signal changes in the conversation's direction; works with partner to explore topics in depth

Interpersonal–Asking for Clarification

Novice			Intermediate			Pre-Advanced
Says "Huh?" or uses gestures and facial expressions to show confusion	Repeats what was not understood; asks speaker to repeat or slow down	Provides perceived meaning; repeats and adds a tag question to show understanding	Asks simple questions to clarify meaning	Provides alternatives, examples, to point out what is not understood; asks for a definition or explanation	Paraphrases to verify what was understood	Adds own interpretation to verify what was understood

Interpersonal–Comprehensibility

Novice		Intermediate			Pre-Advanced	
Sticks to known words	Tries to use new phrases and combinations; rarely successful	Some success in using new phrases and combinations	Some errors that may require repetition to be understood	Control of language decreases as topics and time frames expand beyond present and familiar	Some errors; errors seldom interfere with comprehension	Errors are not noticeable; no interference with comprehension

Presentational–Content

Novice		Intermediate			Pre-Advanced	
Random thoughts put together; jumps from one subtopic to another; no elaboration	Stays on topic, but little organization by subtopics; little elaboration	Clear focus on topic; clear sub-topics; some elaboration	Elaborates on main topic, exploring beyond broad subtopics; makes a point	Uses cohesive devices and transitions to link thoughts, sub-topics, and guide the overall argument (e.g., contrasts, conclusions, contradictions)	Clear overarching point; elaborated with strong examples and elaboration	Creative elements appropriately inserted; uses idioms appropriately and accurately
Predictable content, usually within immediate environment		Shares appropriate and relevant information; offers own opinion, examples, and suggestions			Provides in-depth analysis; provides personal reflection on and connection to topic	

Presentational–Delivery

Novice		Intermediate			Pre-Advanced	
Sticks to highly memorized words, phrases, sentences	Well-rehearsed or edited; sticks to formulaic expres-sions	Begins to self-monitor to correct errors when mov-ing off memorized "text"	Able to rely on notes for spoken presentations and less on memorized "text"	Pacing of spoken presentation fits topic and helps audience	Adjusts voice and style to underscore message	Consciously adjusts register as appropriate

Presentational–Impact

Novice		Intermediate			Pre-Advanced	
Focuses only on successful task completion	Gestures or visuals help audience understand message	Integrates graphic organizer or visual to support meaning	Uses comparison or contrast to reinforce meaning	Personalization maintains audience's atten-tion; weaves in personal stories and examples	Engages audience with some interaction	Varies delivery style to maintain attention

Step Four: Describe the Performance That Exceeds Your Expectations and the Performance That Does Not Meet Your Expectations

An effective rubric will make clear to students how good is good enough. A well-designed rubric will show students the characteristics of the language performance that meet the proficiency target. In order to help students know what they need to do to improve their performance, a rubric also needs to describe the characteristics of the language performance that does not yet meet the proficiency target and the characteristics that exceed the proficiency target. In this way, students can see not only where they are along a continuum of increasing proficiency, but what they need to demonstrate in order to improve. By showing students what they can work on, a rubric has the potential to be more motivating and helpful than a letter or numerical grade.

To be useful as an outline of performance goals for students, the rubric should be based on real performances. If a description uses words like "perfect" or "error-free," students will be discouraged that an excellent performance would never receive the highest ranking if a single error occurred. Considering real student performances, teachers understand that perfect or error-free are not realistic goals, even for native speakers.

A guiding principle for describing the performances below and above "Meets Expectations" is to use the same categories. In Step Three, descriptors were clustered around a key category in the analytic rubric. Those clustered categories now serve to link the descriptions across three, four, or five "levels" of the rubric. In this way, students are guided to see what they need to do to improve their performance, not as a large and overly general category and not just as "more" of something, but as qualitative differences on each of the identified categories.

In order for the rubric to be a tool to push student performance to the next level, it should describe a reasonable increase in quality for the listed criteria. For example, one criterion for evaluating interpersonal communication might be "maintaining and sustaining the conversation." The steps to move from "Does Not Meet Expectations" to "Exceeds Expectations" could be as follows:

Does Not Meet Expectations
- Rarely initiates conversation
- Reacts to questions when asked

Meets Expectations
- Makes effort to initiate conversation by asking questions
- Follows up partner's comments with an appropriate comment or question

Exceeds Expectations
- Takes responsibility to initiate and maintain conversation (asking several questions; using different strategies to get partner to respond)
- Follows up partner's comments with a variety of comments or questions

Students benefit by clear description of what they can do to raise their performance to the next level. Keep in mind that each step should be achievable by students in the class, keeping all descriptions within reach of students. The step from one to the next should also be achievable within a realistic amount of time, so students can get a sense of their progress. When the steps between each level are too great, students will not experience improvement often enough to boost their motivation.

A rubric is motivating to students when the degree of change from one level to the next can be achieved during the period of time that students will be evaluated on it. If the same rubric is used over the course of a semester or year in order to gauge improvement, then the movement from one level to the next should be achievable by students during that period of time. Making a level unattainable is discouraging and an unproductive way to show students how to improve. After writing the descriptors for "Does Not Meet" and "Exceeds Expectations," check that the steps through the various levels of the rubric are of equal size and increment. Make sure the differences between the descriptions do not describe a tiny step and then a giant leap.

When rubrics are designed to show movement over the course of an entire language program, consider the approach of ACTFL's Integrated Performance Assessment (IPA) project. In the IPA Rubrics (see Appendix D), the "Meets Expectations" of the Novice level is used as the "Does Not Meet Expectations" of the Intermediate level. Likewise, the "Exceeds Expectations" of one level can become the "Meets Expectations" of the next.

The same description moves down a notch at each successive proficiency level:

Novice Level: Exceeds Expectations

becomes

Intermediate Level: Meets Expectations

becomes

Pre-Advanced Level: Does Not Meet Expectations

How many "levels" should be described in the rubric? Remember, the rubric is all about helping students improve their language performance. The rubric is not about quantity, but quality. When teachers design rubrics with too many levels, they are challenged to find descriptors to differentiate each level that avoid quantity. When the "slices" get too small, the differences in performance are difficult to describe in terms of quality (such as how well students are maintaining or sustaining the conversation) and tend to focus more on quantity (such as the number of questions students asked). The unintended consequence is to make students hyperaware of counting the various elements of the performance rather than focusing on communication and the messages at the heart of it. Remember to keep the range between the lowest and highest levels to the range of how far students can improve during the period of instruction. The number of levels needed in a rubric is the number that can be described with appropriate differentiation, and not just numbers. In numerous rubric projects, three levels has been a workable and helpful format. Some districts have created shared rubrics with four or five levels in each category. Ex-

periment with what works best for the given performance task and the range of feedback students need at that point in time.

How each level of the rubric is labeled is another way to decide how many levels are needed in the rubric. Descriptive words can help identify the "levels" desired in designing the rubric.[9]

Level	Descriptive Words
Exceeds Expectations	• Exemplary • Excellent • Superior
Meets Expectations	• Strong • Solid • Good
Almost Meets Expectations (Not There Yet)	• Needs Improvement • Too Limited
Minimal Attempt to Meet Expectations	• Inadequate • Insufficient • Unacceptable
No Attempt to Meet Expectations	• Unratable

As teachers, we want our students to note progress. A well-written rubric describes the pathway to improvement. Notice how these guiding principles are applied in the development of the descriptions for "Exceeds Expectations" and "Does Not Meet Expectations" for each of the three modes of communication in the following example, which builds on the "Meets Expectations" level in Step Three.

Example: Presentational Mode Rubric–Language Control

Novice Level

Exceeds Expectations	Meets Expectations	Does Not Meet Expectations
Most accurate when producing simple sentences in present time		

Intermediate Level

Exceeds Expectations	Meets Expectations		Does Not Meet Expectations
	Strong: Most accurate with connected sentence-level discourse in present time	Weak: Most accurate when producing simple sentences in present time	

Pre-Advanced Level

Exceeds Expectations	Meets Expectations	Does Not Meet Expectations
		Most accurate with connected sentence-level discourse in present time

Travel Unit Example–Intermediate Level

Why would I choose a particular destination?		
Interpretive		
Task: Using Internet resources, fill in requested information about the area you have selected to visit in the target country.		
Step Three: Describe the performance that meets your expectations, with identified categories		
• Main idea: Can identify the main ideas of the various Internet resources • Supporting details: Can identify some supporting details • Inferences: Can use context clues to identify meaning of some new words		
Step Four: Describe the performance that exceeds your expectations and the performance that does not meet your expectations		
Exceeds Expectations	**Meets Expectations**	**Does Not Meet Expectations**
Main idea: Identifies the main ideas of all Internet resources used Supporting details: Identifies most of the supporting details to better describe the main ideas Inferences: Uses context clues to identify meaning of many new words	Main idea: Can identify the main ideas of most of the various Internet resources Supporting details: Can identify some supporting details from the text Inferences: Can use context clues to identify meaning of some new words	Main idea: Identifies the main ideas of some of the Internet resources used; some are incorrect or incomplete Supporting details: Identifies the obvious supporting details, those based minimally on the text Inferences: Not able to use context clues to identify meaning of new words

Presentational		
Task: Create a commercial and a flyer to promote the region you have selected.		
Step Three: Describe the performance that meets your expectations, with identified categories		
• Flow and organization: Provides a logical flow, keeping to main point and providing clear subtopics; uses some cohesive devices to help listener/viewer • Delivery: Basic language structures are understandable with little difficulty; voice is clear, loud, little hesitation • Maintain audience's attention: Uses visuals to guide the viewer through the presentation		
Step Four: Describe the performance that exceeds your expectations and the performance that does not meet your expectations		
Exceeds Expectations	**Meets Expectations**	**Does Not Meet Expectations**
Flow and organization: Thoughts hold together as a cohesive paragraph; clear focus on the main point; subtopics provide important details to expand and explore the subtopics; cohesive devices continually guide the listener/viewer Delivery: Understandable with no difficulty; well-rehearsed; voice is consistently clear and loud with little hesitation Maintain audience's attention: Visuals continually support the message and help with comprehension; dramatic language or presentation also maintains audience's attention	Flow and organization: Provides a logical flow, keeping to main point and providing clear subtopics; uses some cohesive devices to help listener/viewer Delivery: Basic language structures are understandable with little difficulty; voice is clear, usually loud enough, little hesitation Maintain audience's attention: Uses visuals to guide the viewer through the presentation	Flow and organization: Writing is a series of sentences with little language to connect thoughts or direct the flow; subtopics are clear but are not elaborated Delivery: Basic language structures are understandable but occasionally difficult to follow; voice is usually loud enough, but with frequent hesitation Maintain audience's attention: Visuals are shown and are partially connected with the presentation

Interpersonal
Task: Discuss with a partner the places in classmates' commercials, deciding which will be the most exciting to visit and how you will convince the rest of your class.
Step Three: Describe the performance that meets your expectations, with identified categories
• Communication strategies: Attempts to maintain and sustain the conversation by asking questions and providing personal responses • Asks for clarification: Uses limited strategies, such as repeating words and sometimes selecting substitute words • Comprehensibility: Uses circumlocution when lacking vocabulary; effectively uses words and simple sentences to make ideas known
Step Four: Describe the performance that exceeds your expectations and the performance that does not meet your expectations

Exceeds Expectations	Meets Expectations	Does Not Meet Expectations
Communication strategies: Takes responsibility to initiate and maintain conversation (asking several questions; using different strategies to get partner to respond); follows up partner's comments with a variety of comments or questions Asks for clarification: Uses several strategies, such as repeating words, rephrasing questions, or modeling an answer Comprehensibility: Uses words, phrases, and sentences to express ideas; uses circumlocution, gestures, and examples to help when lacking vocabulary	Communication strategies: Attempts to maintain and sustain the conversation by asking questions and providing personal responses Asks for clarification: Uses limited strategies, such as repeating words and sometimes selecting substitute words Comprehensibility: Uses circumlocution when lacking vocabulary; effectively uses words and simple sentences to make ideas known	Communication strategies: Rarely initiates conversation; reacts to questions when asked Asks for clarification: Great difficulty in negotiating for clarification (may only ask "What?") Comprehensibility: Uses memorized words and phrases, plus simple sentences; may resort to English when lacking vocabulary

For beginning students, the range in performance is often extremely limited. Trying to break out distinctions becomes an exercise in trying to find slightly different words for very slight changes in performance. A more useful tool may be a checklist. Rather than showing the degree of accomplishment along each criterion, the checklist identifies steps that lead up to improvement while helping both the teacher and student be very clear as to what is expected. The student either can or cannot do what is listed on the checklist. By arranging the checklist items in a way that leads from the most simple and basic to the more complex, students can note their progress as they work to exhibit more and more of the listed characteristics. Phrasing these in student-friendly terms helps students know what they need to do in order to improve.

Sample Checklist:

Task: Novice Level–Interpersonal

Find out who has the busiest schedule.

Performance Criteria	I can do this on my own	I can do this with some help (from a student or the teacher)	I cannot do this
I can use numbers			
I can use words for classes			
I can use words for activities			
I can understand my partner			
I can say how many times, how often, how frequently I have or do various things			
I can ask some questions			
I can provide some description			
I can use expressions to show that I agree or disagree with what my partner says			
I can say how I am feeling (emotions)			

Even at a more advanced level, a checklist provides a framework for helping students know the expectations and how close they come to meeting or exceeding them.

Task: Pre-Advanced Level–Interpersonal

Find out who has the busiest schedule.

Performance Criteria	Achieves the target and more (Consistently)	Achieves the target (Frequently)	Achieves the target (Minimally)	Falls short of the target
Questions include a variety of topics and interests beyond just school				
Many questions are open-ended to encourage more interaction in the conversation				
Questions lead to in-depth exploration of the topic, beyond mere facts; asks for more detail, further explanation				
Demonstrates careful listening by using expressive reactions and appropriate follow-up questions				

DOING IT ON YOUR OWN

Step Four: Describe the Performance that Exceeds Your Expectations and the Performance that Does Not Meet Your Expectations

Thematic focus:
(Example: What makes a good friend? How am I a good friend to others?)

Targeted language level, functions emphasized in this unit:
(Example: Novice–Describe with lists of adjectives or verbs)

Mode of communication:
(Interpretive, interpersonal, or presentational)

Fill in the categories identified in Step Three for "Meets Expectations" in this rubric template. Then for Step Four describe what student language performance would look like in one or two steps prior to meeting your expectations ("Does Not Meet Expectations") and in one or two steps past meeting your expectations ("Exceeds Expectations").

Refer to the scales of sample criteria from Novice to Pre-Advanced–identified by mode of communication (in Step Three, pp. 53-54).

In Step Three, you identified "Meets Expectations" on these scales. Now use the descriptors on either side of your "Meets" to help you describe one or two stages that precede your level of expectation and one or two stages that exceed your level of expectation. These descriptors are designed to help you build your rubric for a specific performance assessment task. The mode of communication is important to consider as that communicative purpose changes the expectations around accuracy and completeness.

Additional help is found in Appendixes B and D (the *ACTFL Performance Guidelines for K–12 Learners* and ACTFL's Integrated Performance Assessment Rubrics).

Exceeds Expectations	Meets Expectations	Does Not Meet Expectations
Using the same criteria as "Meets Expectations," describe the language performance that will meet your expectations in the future (e.g., in one semester)		Using the same criteria as "Meets Expectations," describe the language performance that met your expectations in the past (e.g., back one semester)

Step Five: Pilot with Students and Revise Based on Student Work and Feedback

Rubrics that include quantities (e.g., ask five questions) or adjectives that are difficult to judge (e.g., energetic, acceptable) encourage students to make the case for a re-evaluation of their performance rating or score rather than helping them focus on how to improve. If the rubric lists five questions as "Meets Expectations" and more than five for "Exceeds," students will tend to make sure they ask at least six questions regardless of the need or appropriateness of the questions. Students will also argue what constitutes a question (e.g., is a single word like "Why?" good enough?) and will expect the teacher to accept repeats of questions if not prohibited in the rubric. The first time a rubric is tried out on real students, all of its flaws will surface. Students will ask the probing questions that will show the teacher any loopholes.

Options for piloting with students:

- On a practice activity or formative assessment, use the rubric that will be used for the unit's summative assessment task in the same communication mode.
- Pull out a single criterion of the rubric and use that element to provide feedback to students during a practice activity or formative assessment.
- Try out the same criterion for a week, to see how quickly and easily students understand the descriptors.
- Have students see the rubric, discuss it, and then conduct a practice run with a performance task reflecting what students will do as the summative assessment.
- Ask students to use the rubric to evaluate their own performance and that of their partner (or to use the rubric to provide feedback to classmates they observe performing language tasks that reflect real-life applications).

Then, observe and listen. Watch how students react to the ratings they receive. Listen to how students discuss the rubric with the teacher and with each other. Capture student comments about the rubric, from ease of use to clarity of expectations.

Questions to Ask About the Rubric After Piloting with Students

1. Can the language performance be evaluated during the assessment task?
   - For interpersonal conversations, can the rubric be filled out while the students are having the conversation (or does it take a long time to complete it after the conversation ends)?
   - For presentational tasks, can the rubric be filled out while viewing, reading, or listening to the presentation (or does it require a long time to complete afterwards)?
   - For interpretive assessments, can the rubric be filled out while reading or hearing a student's response to the interpretive prompts (or does it require extensive review of the material being interpreted)?
2. Are the criteria of the rubric the important or essential elements of the performance?
   - Do the right elements get evaluated?
   - Were other important elements noticed in the performance that could not be evaluated under any of the criteria of the rubric?
   - Are unimportant elements counted in the rubric, elements that did not identify any ways that students could improve their language performance?
3. Do the descriptions of each criterion focus on quality and not quantity?
4. Are the descriptors quickly and easily understood by students?
5. Are students able to use the rubric to explain what they need to do to improve their language performance?
6. Are the steps between "Does Not Meet Expectations" and "Meets Expectations" and between "Meets Expectations" and "Exceeds Expectations" parallel, of equal size of improvement, and achievable within a realistic amount of time?
   - Did it feel like "Exceeds Expectations" would be almost impossible to achieve?
   - Was it difficult to distinguish between two ratings on any of the criteria (i.e., were the rating descriptions minimally different or too similar)?[10]

Once the actual performance assessment task is completed, the body of student work provides another powerful lens for evaluating the rubric. A more proactive approach is to locate previous student work samples that are similar to the proposed assessment task. Examining the work samples is an excellent way to evaluate the rubric. First, look at several student samples and place them into three piles that represent lower-than-expected performance (not good enough for the current level of students), expected performance (at the level targeted), and beyond-the-expected performance (containing some elements that really impress). Next, examine each pile and write down

DOING IT ON YOUR OWN

Step Five: Pilot with Students and Revise Based on Student Work and Feedback

Thematic focus:

(Example: What makes a good friend? How am I a good friend to others?)

Targeted language level, functions emphasized in this unit:

(Example: Novice–Describe with lists of adjectives or verbs)

Mode of communication:

(Interpretive, interpersonal, or presentational)

Method of piloting the rubric with students:	Practice activities:	Samples of student work:
Method for eliciting student feedback on the rubric:	Observations:	Discussion:
Revisions to rubric based on piloting and feedback:	Changes to criteria:	Changes to level descriptions:

the criteria that sum up why those work samples are in that pile. Compare the criteria and their descriptions to the rubric designed for the unit assessment tasks. Evaluate the rubric to determine if the right criteria are included and if each level is described with similar terms for the quality of the student work.

Step Six: Determine How You Will Communicate the Assessment Results (Including Using Rubrics in Grades and Incorporating Feedback into Your Instruction)

The process of designing performance assessment tasks and accompanying rubrics has the potential to change the way students are graded. Grades are a means of communicating student achievement. The rubrics for the performance assessment tasks were developed to identify student progress and point the way to improvement. Students, parents, and teachers will give more value to the rubrics when they become part of the grade.

Converting rubrics to grades by using simple numbers or percentages potentially undermines the concept of "Meets Expectations." A natural tendency is to assign numbers in a variety of ways such as in the chart below.

The student rated as "Exceeds Expectations" in all three categories receives 9 points out of a possible 9, for 100%. The student rated as "Meets Expectations" in all three categories receives 6 points out of a possible 9, for 66.67%. The student rated as "Does Not Meet Expectations" in all three categories receives 3 points out of a possible 9, for 33.34%. In a typical grading scheme 90–100% earns an A, 80–89% earns a B, 70–79% earns a C, and 60–69% earns a D. In this case, the student meeting the expectations in each category has 66.67% or a D—definitely not the message a teacher wants to send to students!

Changing the numbers to 5-3-1 or another formula still results in this problem. The challenge is to make sure that when students meet the expectations, they do not receive a grade labeled as poor.

To counter this unintended consequence, some teachers have developed conversion charts that change rubric scores into grades by starting a completed performance at already a 60% or higher score. The rationale is that a completed performance is already not failing. For many teachers, fully meeting expectations is represented by a grade of B, exceeding expectations is represented by a grade of A, and not fully achieving expectations is represented on a scale of C to F.

In the example above, the possible scores range from 3 to 9. The ratings added to 60% could be set up as follows:

3 = 65% = D
4 = 70% = C-
5 = 76% = C
6 = 82% = B-
7 = 88% = B+
8 = 94% = A
9 = 100% = A+

The rationale is that the student who receives all "Does Not Meet Expectations" ratings would begin with 60% and then add a value to go above the 60% line. A student earning all "Meets Expectations" ratings would end up with a B-. The student earning all "Exceeds Expectations" ratings would end up with an A+. The increments for each increase in the rubric score result in an increase of six percentage points. This is but one scheme for developing grades based on rubric scores. The message to emphasize must be that the rubric is about the quality of the language performance and not about counting elements of the performance. Any conversion to a grade must be done with caution and a carefully developed rationale and process.

	Exceeds Expectations	Meets Expectations	Does Not Meet Expectations
Content	3	2	1
Delivery	3	2	1
Impact	3	2	1

Another approach is to use rubrics in the calculation of a quarter or semester grade, not to convert the rubric itself into a grade. Quarter or semester grades are usually based on various categories, such as homework, tests and quizzes, a large project, and class participation. The rubrics provide evidence that can influence the grade in a given category. For example, categories could be added related to the standards: interpretive, interpersonal, and presentational. The rubrics used during the course of the quarter or semester could then be used to influence the grade in one of these categories, based on student improvement as shown by the various rubrics used during the quarter or semester. Rewarding improvement is important and motivating, so isn't improvement a valid element to include in a grade? The rubrics can be evaluated by looking for improvement on various criteria as well as overall. A student who shows improvement would be rewarded by adjusting the percentage, raw number, or letter grade based on that element.[11] For example, if a student's scores on assessments of interpersonal communication generated a B (e.g., 82%), the teacher looking at the three interpersonal assessment rubrics could adjust that quarter's interpersonal score by the size of improvement noted. If the rubrics moved from the "Meets Expectations" to more consistently in the "Exceeds Expectations," then the B could become a B+ or even an A-. A percentage adjustment could also be used based on degree of improvement. The 82% interpersonal "score" could be adjusted by adding five percentage points for some movement upward and eight percentage points for having consistently moved up to the "Exceeds Expectations" rating. This is but one example of how such adjustments could be made.

Rubrics can also provide a critical element for evaluating a portfolio. Rather than just collecting performance evidence, the well-designed rubric gives students and the teacher the set of objective criteria that allow the student work to become part of the quarter or semester grade.

To give value to the rubrics, the teacher must decide on a system of using them as part of the quarter or semester grade. This provides a balance to any other elements that are part of the grade. The inclusion of rubrics ensures balance in what is valued. This will make the goal of improvement on the assessment rubrics important to students, leading to stronger attention to doing well on the performance tasks.

Ultimately, the rubrics help students know what is important in learning a language. Accuracy is important, but it is not the only criterion. The rubric rewards students for taking risks with language and for having strategies to deal with the lack of comprehension or comprehensibility that may result.

In the end, rubrics change the conversations teachers have with other language teachers. No longer is the focus on being on the same page or in the same chapter or finishing the textbook by the end of the academic year. Teacher conversations move to how to prepare students to do well on common performance assessments and rubrics. Rubrics with clear descriptions of "Meets Expectations" help teachers discuss their instructional targets with other teachers of the same level and guide conversations to improve vertical articulation.

Fairfax County Public Schools (VA) developed an excellent resource to help language teachers design effective rubrics, standardize the expectations and evaluation of each element, and grapple with the conversion of such rubrics into grading schemes. Elements of the Performance Assessment for Language Students (PALS) can be found online at http://www.fcps.edu/DIS/OHSICS/forlang/PALS/rubrics/index.htm.

Step Six: Determine How You Will Communicate the Assessment Results (Including Using Rubrics in Grades and Incorporating Feedback into Your Instruction)

Thematic focus:

(Example: What makes a good friend? How am I a good friend to others?)

Targeted language level, functions emphasized in this unit:

(Example: Novice–Describe with lists of adjectives or verbs)

Mode of communication:

(Interpretive, interpersonal, or presentational)

Method of communicating the assessment results with students:	How will the rubric be used in grading the individual task?	How will the rubric be used in determining the quarter or semester grade?

Thoughts on using percentages to convert rubrics to letter grades:

Thoughts on using rubrics as an element to influence the quarter or semester grade in a category:

Chapter 5: Engaging, Motivating, and Involving Students

Getting Students Involved and Motivated

1. Build student motivation through implementation of performance assessment

   ✓ Engage students through the topics of the performance tasks

   ✓ Engage students by the activities leading to the performance tasks

2. Involve students in the design of rubrics

   ✓ Link the rubric to real-world expectations

   ✓ Understand the expectations as captured in assessment

3. Focus students on their learning

   ✓ Use rubrics and feedback to help students set goals for improvement

   ✓ Develop students' skills for assessing their own performance and progress

Changing a system is not easy. Students have learned how to work the education system. They are accustomed to "earning" a grade based on an accumulation of points. In the author's experience and affirmed through discussion with other teachers, students expect to earn points for completing homework, for quizzes, for tests, for projects, and sometimes even for participating in class. They seem to accept that some of these categories receive more points than others in a system of weighting the grades to reward more challenging work (e.g., tests or a major project). Teachers also report that increasingly not only students, but their parents, too, expect schools to function the way they did for them when success came from accumulating points on the various accepted forms of showing what one had learned. In this environment, teachers now might find it useful to engage students proactively in creating changes to the system in order to help them and their parents learn to value and trust a new system. Teachers may need to make clear the reasons for making the change to basing evaluation and a grade on achieving the expected goals, rather than accumulating points for merely completing the assigned task. One approach is to share why the change is occurring, demonstrate how students will benefit, and make students partners in their own learning.

What Insights on Engaging and Motivating Students Are Implied from Research?

Engaging Students in Their Learning Improves the Learning:

- Shrum and Glisan (2005) describe Vygotsky's concept of the Zone of Proximal Development (ZPD) as both "a tool for learning language and the result of using language with others" (p. 24), with an application to involving students in decisions about the learning, rather than only using curriculum or text materials to determine this.

- Donato (2004) describes the ZPD as a way of understanding the power of language learning when learners use it in collaborative interaction.

- McCafferty (2002) concludes that the ZPD results in learning when language is used in meaningful and purposeful interactions.

- Johnson and Johnson (1987) in their research on cooperative learning identify numerous benefits of group and pair work, including greater achievement and retention.

Motivation Positively Influences Learning:

- Masgoret and Gardner (2003) describe motivation as highly influential in language learning.

- Dörnyei (1994) identifies several factors contributing to student motivation, including the interest and engagement of learning tasks.

- Gardner (1985) shows that when motivated, language learners put forth greater effort and achieve greater success in developing language proficiency.

- Wen (1997) concludes that learners expend more effort when they believe the experience will lead to meaningful results.

- Oxford and Shearin (1994) describe motivation as influenced by the relevance of the goals of a course, the learner's ability to self-evaluate, and the type of assistance and feedback provided by the teacher.

Feedback Should Lead to Student Reflection on Learning:

- Lapkin, Swain, and Smith (2002) suggest that following collaborative tasks teachers discuss with students how they communicated, to clear up language problems.

- Donato and McCormick (1994) describe a portfolio as useful to help students reflect on their language learning by setting goals, choosing strategies to improve, and gathering evidence of the impact of those strategies.

Build Student Motivation Through Implementation of Performance Assessment

Engage Students Through the Topics of the Performance Tasks

During an official Oral Proficiency Interview (OPI), the tester asks the candidate various questions aimed at identifying personal likes and dislikes, hobbies, and general areas of interest. The tester seeks to identify motivating content that will serve to engage the candidate in providing extended description, telling personal stories, and even asking questions of the tester. Without content of personal interest, the tester has a more difficult time gathering a ratable sample. With a prompt that asks the candidate to draw on personal interests, he or she may be more motivated to demonstrate the best performance possible.

The same principle applies to setting an instructional focus in the language classroom. What motivates students to want to engage in classroom activities? Connecting with student personal interests more strongly engages students in the communication tasks. Emphasizing accuracy to the point that it overrides the desire to communicate has a paralyzing effect on students and limits their use of language. A thematic focus is one means to create a need to communicate and maintain student interest in communicating. To move from mere vocabulary topics to an engaging thematic focus, identify areas of student interest within the traditional topic. From the areas of student interest, define a question that will serve to focus the unit of instruction beyond simply being a vocabulary list or a grammar topic. Such a motivating question provides students with many avenues to explore within the topic. Teachers then plan their units of instruction around the focus questions.

Traditional Topic	Areas of Student Interest	Focus Question
Elementary school example: Neighborhood	• What people do "at work" • What buildings are found in the neighborhood	• What makes me feel "at home" in my neighborhood? • What would make me feel comfortable in a neighborhood in another country?
Middle school example: Food	• Where food comes from • How to cook (hands-on)	• What makes my diet healthy? • Are healthy diets the same in every culture?
High school example: Leisure activities	• What teenagers do in their free time • Hobbies, sports, music • What activities fill free time in a culture	• What makes my day busy? • How would my day be different in another culture?

Consider how these traditional topics could be changed to better engage students by linking with areas of student interests and providing a reason to be engaged in the tasks, rather than just to learn vocabulary and grammatical structures.

Identifying a focus for a unit of instruction provides continuity for the various learning activities. Not only are vocabulary and grammatical structures reinforced by the repetition of the thematic content, but students continually build on what they knew prior to the start of the unit, adding more knowledge, developing new insights, and becoming better able to articulate their own ideas to share with others. In order to maintain this interest, the thematic focus needs to tap student curiosity on the topic and must generate their interest in interpreting, discussing, and presenting their ideas.

Engage Students by the Activities Leading to the Performance Tasks

Do students need information in an interpretive task for a purpose other than just for the assessment? In the author's experience, students only do exactly what is asked on the assessment, rarely surprising the teacher by digging deeper or by contributing more than what is requested. Purposeful activities build on the curiosity and "need to know" set up in the unit's thematic focus.

Motivate students by providing clear learning targets—and clear purposes behind the tasks. How well can adults watch the evening news and then complete a 10-point multiple-choice quiz with any degree of accuracy or success? Without a clear purpose for watching the evening news, the viewer does not know what is important, what should be the area of focus, or what should be remembered. The viewer will have much more success when the purpose is identified prior to watching. Then the viewer watches the news in order to achieve the identified goal, such as re-telling a favorite story; identifying the most important world, state, and local items; or comparing the coverage of a story from different news sources or its development over time.

Performance assessments focus the instructional activities toward a clear communicative purpose. The various learning activities during the unit of instruction will be leading toward successful performance in the interpretive, interpersonal, and presentational modes of communication. If the performance assessments require an application of the vocabulary and grammatical structures students are learning, teachers must develop increasingly independent use of those language elements through the daily experiences provided in their language classes. If students need to ask questions in the interpersonal performance assessment task, then the teacher designs activities so students practice asking questions. If students need to skim material in the interpretive performance assessment task, in order to pull out the main idea and key details, then the teacher models the thinking that goes into this process while leading students through an example. This occurs in highly structured ways at the beginning of the unit, but moves to less teacher direction and more student responsibility as students build their confidence to ask questions or skim on their own.

Consider developing student skills in a given mode of communication: interpretive, interpersonal, or presentational. During the unit of instruction, what is the flow of activities that work from tightly focused learning activities to scaffolded practice of skills toward more and more independent applications of those skills? Keep the flow of development in mind while guid-

Travel Unit Example–Intermediate Level

Motivating Focus Question: Why would I choose a particular destination? Engaging Performance Task–Interpersonal: Discuss with a partner the places in a classmates' commercials, explaining which you want to visit and why.	Language Goals: • Give more extended description • State opinion and provide evidence to support it • Ask questions to initiate and extend discussion

Sample Practice Activities Within the Thematic Focus:
• Information gap pair activities (each partner looks at a different travel photo, identifying what they have in common, to decide if they are from the same country).
• Students look at a tourist website for a travel destination and identify all they would want to do in that location.
• Students form pairs and have one minute to share what they like to do when visiting a new location. After one minute, students form new pairs and continue their conversation. The goal is to expand students' ideas on what they might do and practice ways to describe different options.
• Small groups each read about one destination and prepare to make the case as to why the whole class should visit that destination. Groups are re-formed, with representatives from each of the small groups in each of the re-formed groups. The new task is to come to consensus on where the whole class should go, stating the case for their destination, but looking for commonalities among the destinations, such as outdoor activities, arts activities, or adventures.

DOING IT ON YOUR OWN

Unit thematic focus:

Identify the motivating focus question for the topic:

Describe the language goals for one mode of communication during this unit of instruction:
(*Interpretive, interpersonal, or presentational*)

Identify a variety of practice activities to engage and motivate students, working toward more and more independent performance of the targeted mode of communication:

ing students toward the language performance goal of the unit of instruction. These formative learning checks and practice assessments are critical to prepare students for the summative assessment of the unit.

Involve Students in the Design of Rubrics

The assessment tasks should engage students by connecting with their interests. Another tool to engage, involve, and motivate students is to make clear the expected level of language performance. When the Wisconsin Department of Public Instruction rolled out its curriculum guide[1], teachers involved in piloting the backward design process reported that when students knew the parameters of the language sample they needed to produce and how it was going to be evaluated, they were more motivated to learn the language elements that would help them produce a high quality of that language sample. Knowing what is expected gives students a reason to spend time practicing the vocabulary and language structures they will need for the performance task.

Link the Rubric to Real-World Expectations

To help students understand what is expected, involve them in the design of the assessment task's rubrics. Start from the same beginning point as for the design of the task: What are the characteristics of this language performance in the real world? The task reflects what people do in purposeful communication and so, too, the rubric should reflect the qualities that matter in the real context. For example, what matters most in conversations is expressing one's point and engaging the other person in the topic. Accuracy and complete sentences help, but are not of primary concern in the speaker's mind. When accuracy falters and hinders communication, strategies for dealing with the resulting miscommunication are essential. Remember the native speakers who said that they focused on the message and not on how it was being conveyed. Mirroring these same criteria from real-world conversations, the teacher's rubric should provide feedback on engaging and maintaining interest in the conversation and strategies to deal with communication breakdown.

In the classroom, the teacher might consider asking students what is valued in real-world communication situations similar to the types they will be doing in the unit's performance assessment tasks. As students describe what is effective in various interpretive, interpersonal, and presentational tasks in school, at home, with friends, in the community, or at work, they start to identify the characteristics of language and use them to form the basis of the rubrics for assessing their language performance in class. The teacher can make the link to the *ACTFL Performance Guidelines for K–12 Learners* by showing the questions that are answered by the descriptions in the rubric:

Comprehensibility: How well is the student understood? (interpersonal and presentational modes only)

Comprehension: How well does the student understand? (interpersonal and interpretive modes only)

Language Control: How accurate is the student's language?

Vocabulary: How extensive and applicable is the student's vocabulary?

Cultural Awareness: How is the student's cultural knowledge reflected in language use?

Communication Strategies: How does the student maintain communication?

Understand the Expectations as Captured in Assessment

Another process for involving students is in refining the language of the rubric. The process is to have students explain in their own words the expected level of performance. By asking guiding questions, the teacher can get students to explore what is meant by the sometimes-technical language of a rubric. Also helpful is to ask students what advice they would give one another in order to achieve the rubric rating they are describing. Consider how the description on the next page of the Intermediate proficiency level for the interpersonal mode might be "translated" by students into language clearer to most teenagers.

Ask students how they interpret the rubric descriptions. Assign small groups of students different elements of the rubric to put into their own words. Ask that students also provide an example of the language that would exhibit the characteristic they had just described. This provides the teacher with a check on students' understanding of the expected level of performance. Involving students in unwrapping the meaning of a rubric is a powerful tool to engage students in their own learning. Take time to plan how to bring students into a deeper understanding of the rubric and how to practice the rubric through various activities leading up to the summative performance assessment tasks of the unit.

IPA Rubric Intermediate (Strong)–Interpersonal Mode	Student Translation into Their Language
Creates with language; ability to express own meaning expands in quantity and quality	It's OK to try to say something you have never said before. Try to put ideas into words that you know in the language to describe what you are thinking–even when you don't have the exact words. You should add more words, phrases, and sentences and be more correct.
Maintains conversation by asking and answering questions	You don't just wait until someone asks you a question, but you ask questions to get others talking and to keep the conversation going. Make sure your questions and the information that you share stick to the topic and explore it further.
Most accurate with connected sentence-level discourse in present time	It should not be difficult to put several sentences together when talking about things in the present. Everyone should understand you pretty well. Don't be afraid to use other tenses, but don't obsess about being perfect because you won't be! Just keep trying to make the other person understand what you are saying.

Travel Unit Example

Presentational Task *Create a commercial and a flyer to showcase the region selected to visit, matching personal interests.*		
Real World Characteristics **(generated by students)**	**Emerging Rubric** **(categories)**	**Student Description of the** **Rubric Categories**
Grabs attention	Impact: Grabs and maintains interest of audience	Impact: Images catch your eye; big ideas and images are shown graphically and repeated; images reinforce what is being said; shows all the things that the target audience would like to do there.
Visuals keep the viewer interested		
Language is kept short and to the point	Information: Complete, direct, and presented in memorable way(s)	Information: Just enough details are given to help viewer remember them; big ideas provide enough convincing evidence to make viewer want to go there.
Many reasons are given to visit the region and all are connected with what people would want to do there		

Focus Students on Their Learning

Use Rubrics and Feedback to Help Students Set Goals for Improvement

Taking time to understand and practice the rubric allows students time to identify the area or areas where they need improvement, before it is too late to improve. When students know from the beginning the criteria on which they will be evaluated, throughout the unit they can be led to reflect on what it takes to be successful in the assessment. The time given to understand expectations and for students to evaluate where they are on that scale is time well spent, time that makes the learning activities more productive.

When students are involved in designing the rubric, they start to take responsibility for their learning. When expectations, such as grading criteria, are kept secret, students find it more difficult to take responsibility for their learning. Teachers understandably are upset when students say that the teacher "gave" them the grade, but until students are clear on what counts, they have no other explanation. When engaged in identifying key criteria, describing them in their own words, and envisioning examples of the language that the rubric descriptors represent, students are empowered to take charge of their own improvement.

Help Students Become Familiar with the Rubrics

To engage students in their own learning and to help them focus on what they need to improve, the rubric should be shared early in the unit. Letting students know up front what is expected is both fair and a way to engage students in their learning. Another advantage for the teacher is that by sharing the rubric early in the unit, students will ask about items that are unclear, ambiguous, redundant, or not measurable. The teacher can explain them or change the rubric. Doing so prior to the actual assessment is extremely beneficial to both students and teacher.

Practice the Rubric with Students

One strategy is to focus on one criterion of the rubric for a certain period of time—a class period or a week—in order to limit what students are thinking about while practicing the communication task. The teacher needs to take advantage of assessable moments in the classroom, designing opportunities for formative assessment and then focusing feedback while listening to the student conversations. The teacher might announce that this week the focus during interpersonal communication activities will be on strategies to maintain conversation by asking appropriate questions and following up on the topic. While engaged in pair activities, students will be practicing multiple aspects of language, but the teacher might circulate and provide feedback on this one criterion to some of the pairs during the activity. The teacher might use the same rubric descriptors and simply circle the performance each student exhibited as the teacher was listening. The next day, in another pair activity, the teacher can listen to pairs of students not evaluated the first day on the same criterion. In this way, students begin to internalize the expectations of the rubric descriptions.

Provide Feedback as Part of Instruction

Feedback is essential to improve student performance. Blended into each day's instruction, a teacher's feedback guides students to reflect on their performances, focusing on what was effective and what was not effective in the effort to communicate. In the classroom, such feedback takes many informal forms. In the IPA project, teachers in the pilot sites reported on their increased awareness of the type of feedback they provided their students and the strong impact on student awareness of what they needed to do to improve their performance. The feedback loop is an excellent opportunity to assist student understanding of the interpretive text before they go to the next performance assessment. Feedback following the interpersonal task helps students evaluate their own use of critical communication strategies. Additionally, if the teacher provides

responsive assistance (i.e., responses that help students identify their errors and self-correct) during the feedback loop, students can gain a better understanding of how to improve their performance.

Teachers need to make a conscious decision when providing feedback: Will the discussion of the strategies students are using as they approach the performance assessment tasks occur in the students' native language or the target language? The decision should center around which language will allow the teacher and the students to explore the mental strategies students are using to make meaning and express it. If students are able to have this conversation in the target language, class time is maximized to provide language practice as well as analysis of student thinking. If students are not able to have this conversation in the target language, the teacher may make an instructional decision that a few minutes in English to help students improve their language skills by making them conscious of their meaning-making strategies will be worthwhile.

An Example of Feedback[2]

Learners bring two levels of cognitive development when faced with problem-solving tasks: an actual level (i.e., tasks which they can perform unassisted); and a potential developmental level, which denotes what students may be able to do with assistance. Vygotsky defines the zone of proximal development (ZPD) as "the distance between the learner's actual developmental level as determined by independent problem-solving (unassisted performance) and the level of potential development as determined through problem-solving under adult guidance or more capable peers (assisted performance)."[3]

As Vygotsky reminds us: "Teaching is effective only when it *awakens and rouses to life those functions which are in a stage of maturing, which lie in the zone of proximal development. Teaching must be aimed not so much at the ripe, but at the ripening functions.*"[4]

What does this look like? After correcting the student responses on an interpretive performance assessment, the teacher now

---

Note: This chapter reproduces material directly from the Integrated Performance Assessment Manual. See Endnotes on p. 89 for page numbers.

Glisan, E., Adair-Hauck, B., Koda, K., Sandrock, P., & Swender, E. (2003). *ACTFL integrated performance assessment.* Alexandria, VA: The American Council on the Teaching of Foreign Languages.

understands which tasks the students can perform by themselves, and which tasks are challenging and require responsive assistance on the part of the teacher. For example, after correcting the interpretive responses, the teacher may notice that many of the students did well on two sections of the Intermediate-level tasks: main idea and supporting details. However, students may not have performed nearly as well on the "guessing meaning from context" tasks. Enlightened with this critical information, the teacher has a rich opportunity for an instructional interaction within the students' "zone of proximal development" (ZPD) during the feedback loop. Using assisting questions and cognitive probes,[5] the teacher guides students to become more aware of the various reading strategies that may be used to solve interpretive tasks. The feedback loop will be more beneficial and productive if the teacher provides cognitively challenging, responsive assistance, rather than explicit feedback.[6] The following two protocols highlight the differences between *explicit* and *responsive* teacher feedback.

Explicit Teacher Feedback

(T) *Most of you had difficulty with Section III, "Guessing Meaning from Context." We'd better go over these. Who knows the answer to Question 1, "en allumant"? It can be found in the first paragraph. Jeff?*

(S1) *I didn't get that one.*

(T) *OK. Susan?*

(S2) *I think it means "opening."*

(T) *No, it doesn't mean "opening." "En ouvrant" means "while opening." That's in the sentence above. Trevor, you did well on this section. What's your answer?*

(S3) *I put down "while lighting."*

(T) *Correct. It comes from the verb "allumer," which means "to light" or, in this case, "turn on or light the lamps." OK. Let's go on to number 2. Annie?*

(S4) *I didn't get that one.*

(T) *OK. Sam?*

Responsive and Scaffolded Teacher Feedback to Improve Student Performance

(T) *Most of the class had difficulty with Section III, "Guessing Meaning from Context." This is a difficult section, and that is why it is considered to be a task that falls into the "Exceeds Expectations" category. But if you want to become better readers, we need to have strategies for guessing meaning from context. Let's try to figure out how to solve these "guessing meaning from context" questions so that you'll do better the next time.*

Look at question 1, "en allumant," which is in the first paragraph. How can we try to guess the meaning of that word? First, think to yourselves about some ways that you can make an educated guess about the meaning of this word. (Give students some time to reflect on possible strategies.)

OK. Any suggestions on how we can guess the meaning of this word? Julie?

(S1) *I looked at the picture right next to that paragraph. It's morning time. The woman is opening the curtain; she's letting in the sunlight.*

(T) *Yes. Good strategy. There's a picture to support your understanding and to help you understand the meaning of this paragraph.*

Other suggestions for ways to find the answer? Ray?

(S2) *I think it's a verb. It looks like a verb.*

(T) *Good clue. Yes, it is a verb, and if it's a verb, it's referring to what, Ray?*

(S2) *Oh, an action, a verb refers to some sort of action.*

(T) *Yes. What makes you think that it's a verb or action word, Ray?*

(S2) *It's preceded by the little word "en" just like "en ouvrant," which is in the same sentence. I know "en ouvrant" means "while opening," but I'm not sure of "en allumant."*

(T)   We're on the right track. It's definitely a verb or an action word. There's still another reading strategy that can help us solve this question. What else can we do to try to guess the meaning of the new words, besides looking at the pictures and figuring out the part of speech? Jake?

(S3)   I looked at the other words in the sentence: "en allumant les halogens." I know that "halogènes" means "lights" or "lamps" in English—and it makes sense "to light" or "turn on the lamps" in the morning.

(T)   Exactly. You looked at the other words in the sentence and guessed what would make sense from those contextual clues. We're starting to understand that there are multiple ways to try to guess the meanings of these words. I'm curious, too. Do any of you see a connection between a word in the subtitle and "en allumant"? Larry?

(S4)   "Lumineuse" and "allumant"?

(T)   Yes, that's it. Now what's the connection?

(S4)   They both have the stem "lum."

(T)   Good—and can anyone think of an English word with "lum" that we use frequently around the holidays?

(SS)   A few students respond in unison, "Luminaries!"

(T)   Great. You're catching on. Now, let's try number 2. First, take a minute to reflect and see if you can find the meaning of the word: "tartiné." Share your predictions with a neighbor.

The explicit feedback protocol exemplifies a didactic or "automatic" exchange with questions that mainly assess student knowledge. With these types of questions, students are given little opportunity to improve their performance from the feedback. On the other hand, the responsive feedback protocol represents joint problem-solving on the part of the teacher and learners. To do so, the teacher scaffolds the task by using both assisting as well as assessing questions. "Assisting questions in-

quire in order to produce a cognitive operation that the learner cannot or will not produce alone. The assistance provided by the question prompts the mental operation."[7] "Assessing questions inquire to discover the student's ability to perform without assistance (e.g., to establish what the students may remember from yesterday's lesson)."[8]

Develop Student Skills for Assessing Their Own Performance and Progress

Students need practice and guidance to accurately assess their own performance. Student self-reflection has not been a traditional component in most classrooms. How can students learn to self-assess their current level of performance, determine what they need to do to improve, and then evaluate that improvement?

One way is to share the learning targets with students at the beginning of each unit. Use the performance assessment tasks as those learning targets, along with the criteria on which students will be evaluated. This is the road map for learning that students need. Posting this in the classroom keeps everyone focused on the learning targets. These targets might also be shared in the class syllabus or in a summary form with parents and administrators. The performance targets are a much more motivating set of goals for students than a syllabus of vocabulary and grammar items. The performance targets describe a purposeful use of the language elements learned, identifying the ends and not just the means.

How might students learn to focus on their own performance? Teachers should use practice activities as true warm-ups for the summative assessment tasks. Examining student performance on the practice activities is an opportunity to show students their strengths and areas needing improvement. Then students could be asked to review their recent performances and feedback, either during a brief reflection period weekly or biweekly in class or as homework. Students could compare their performance to the unit's assessment tasks and rubrics. Knowing where they are today, students can be led to identify where they need to improve during the remaining days or weeks of the unit.

Once students have reflected on their own performance, they might be asked to share their feedback with another student. Students should be asked to share not only their reflections, but also the evidence on which those reflections are based.

Students benefit from identifying evidence of their strengths and areas for improvement and then asking someone else to provide verifying evidence by stating what was observed in the students' classroom performance.

A set of performance criteria for an entire language program also provides a means to guide student self-evaluation. Unit-level rubrics are very focused and present smaller steps for improvement, appropriately identifying the progress that students would make in the course of a unit, quarter, or semester. Program-level rubrics, such as the *ACTFL Performance Guidelines for K–12 Learners* or LinguaFolio, describe a larger grain size that requires more time to move from one level to the next. Occasionally students need to see and understand the expectations at the level above that targeted in their current class, not to frustrate them, but to help them see the bigger picture. Students often ask how long it takes to become "fluent" in the language. A set of program-level criteria demonstrates that the answer lies in setting targets that can be achieved within the designated period of time for the class. Program criteria make it clear that once class learning targets are achieved, new targets are in place. Learning a language is a lifelong endeavor!

Student-led conferences are an excellent tool to help students assess their own performance and identify their progress. To prepare for a student-led conference with parents, students engage in regular review of the evidence of what they have learned. Students keep track of their progress related to the goals of the unit and the course. Unit-level rubrics provide a useful vehicle for tracking this progress. For the conference, students should clearly identify the evidence they used to place their performance on the rubric. Looking at strengths and areas needing improvement, students should also identify one or two things to do in the next quarter or semester that will lead to higher ratings on the rubrics. These practices identified for improvement should be specific in describing what the student will do, avoiding quantities or terms like "less" or "more." Students will find a practice session with another student very useful, providing the opportunity to make the case for how the student is doing and showcasing the evidence that led to that conclusion. With this preparation, students are ready to discuss their learning with their parents. Imagine high school students having a significant conversation with their parents regarding what they are learning, not the usual discussion of school that occurs when a student gets home at the end of a school day.

Make the Target Transparent

A transparent performance assessment is more likely to motivate and engage students in the learning process. By designing backward from standards to specific tasks to the evaluation criteria, the teacher is developing a road map for both teaching and learning. By capturing the real goals for instruction in terms of a detailed description of what students are actually expected to do as a result of the instruction, the teacher is targeting the unit and daily lesson plans and is helping the students know what they are supposed to learn and why. The performance assessment tasks provide focus and motivation. If the teacher keeps the target clearly in mind throughout the preparation of a unit and the daily teaching plans, clearly the students will benefit because each activity, each interaction, each question, and each learning check will be focused on what the students need in order to be successful on that assessment task. Such targets guide instruction, but also guide students in their efforts. Rather than guessing what might be on the test and how they will be evaluated, students who know up front how they will be expected to demonstrate what they have learned will get much more out of each class period. Knowing the target, students will know what they need to get out of each activity, know how well they need to be able to do something, and know the language needed to be successful.

Chapter 6: | Impacting Instruction and Program Articulation Through Performance Assessments

Using Performance Assessments to Enhance Programs

- Identify how students will demonstrate progress toward essential targets across levels, schools, and the district-wide program
- Use performance assessments to focus curriculum design
- Use performance assessment feedback to focus design of instructional units and daily lessons
- Develop district- or department-wide performance assessments through an ongoing process of review and refinement

With so many advantages for using performance assessment tasks and well-constructed rubrics, what is preventing teachers from adopting this approach? Making change in isolation is overwhelming; making change in collaboration with other teachers goes a long way to alleviate the anxiety of change.

In recent workshops conducted by the author, teachers most commonly mentioned the following frustrations with current assessment practices:

- **Frustration of Time:** Teachers want to assess student performance but fear the amount of time it will take to administer and to score such an assessment.
- **Fear of Subjectivity:** Evaluating performance relies on criteria that are difficult to describe and often have subtle differences in what exceeds expectations, meets expectations, or does not meet expectations.
- **Challenge of Coming to Consensus:** Teacher standards may vary, as may their emphasis on teaching to different skills or learning targets, thus creating the challenge of preparing students for a next course when teachers lack common criteria for their current levels.

Collaboration among teachers is showing strong potential to address these frustrations. A district-wide system of performance assessment is possible when teachers share efficient practices for administering and evaluating performance assessments, develop rubrics with clear and regular increases in expectations, and identify common goals across a program.

Identify How Students Will Demonstrate Progress Toward Essential Targets Across Levels, Schools, and District-Wide Programs

In one district[1], the ninth grade Spanish teachers designed a test of what their students had learned. Their goal was to prove to the 10th grade teachers that their students had indeed mastered the curriculum. The ninth grade staff faithfully looked

What Insights on the Benefits of Teacher Collaboration Are Implied from Research?

- Goddard, Goddard, and Tschannen-Moran (2007), in a study of teacher collaboration in a large urban school district in the Midwest, reported preliminary support for teacher collaboration on curriculum, instruction, and professional development as a means to improve student achievement.
- A team of researchers that developed a U.S. Department of Education practice guide (Herman, et al., 2008) identify teacher collaboration as an approach embedded in the culture of schools showing dramatic turnaround in student achievement in three years. Promising practices included teams of teachers analyzing student work against standards, identifying common targets for improving instruction, and planning professional development to align lessons across grade levels.
- Horn (2006) reports on several studies and her own research showing that student achievement improved when teachers "collectively examined and revised lessons and rehearsed and refined teaching strategies." (p. 3)
- Blythe, Allen, and Schieffelin (2007) show that when educators engage in a collaborative process to examine student work, they can identify the effectiveness of their instruction, more accurately understand student learning, create more effective curriculum and assessment, and outline strategies that assist students in improving the quality of their work.

at all the items listed in the curriculum: a list of vocabulary categories and grammar items. They designed the test with numerous multiple-choice items to test what their students knew about what they had taught. The ninth grade teachers used this test as the final exam for the year, and then eagerly looked at the student scores. Their good idea turned into a disaster. They were embarrassed to share the results at the meeting they had planned with the 10th grade teachers. The celebration to prove that their students had learned the curriculum turned into a deep analysis of what the results revealed. The students showed with their scores that expecting the same level of performance that they showed on quizzes and chapter tests was unrealistic at the end of the year. The ninth grade teachers had the evidence in their grade books that their students knew the vocabulary and grammar items at an earlier point in time, but when asked to produce evidence of their learning in the same way at a later date, students taught their teachers more about how learning really occurs. The students knew some of the general concepts, but very few of the exceptions. They could identify basic past tense forms, but not the irregular preterite forms! The ninth grade teachers quickly decided not to show this test to the 10th grade teachers and started to design a better way of showcasing what students were able to do with their new language.

Lessons Learned for Informing the Teacher of the Next "Level" or for Creating a Mechanism for Placement into a Program

Sometimes the teacher needs to find out where students are along the continuum of developing proficiency in using the target language. This may be for a cohort group of students, such as a group moving from middle school to high school or moving from a second-year course to a third-year course. This may also be for new students who have different backgrounds in learning languages. In each case, the teacher needs to know the proficiency levels of the incoming students in order to know where to target instruction, both individually and for the group. The assessment strategy does not need to cover everything that has been taught previously, but it needs to cover the key characteristics of each of the proficiency levels. The assessment needs to provide students the opportunity to show what they can do in increasingly sophisticated tasks so that the strengths and weaknesses of each student's profile will be captured. From this profile, students can be well-matched to a program or the instruction can be well-matched to the students.

How does one go about this? Start by identifying those goals that are the application of the specific elements of the district's program or grade-level curriculum. Rather than assessing at this summative level the minutiae of language, assess the communicative goals. State those goals in clear and measurable terms, so that the teacher of the next level does not demand evidence of each vocabulary category or grammar item, but rather looks for evidence of what students can do to show their communication skills: interpretive, interpersonal, or presentational. For example, identify as the interpretive goal for the end of the second year of instruction that students will be able to understand the main idea and some supporting details of a magazine article well supported by its graphic organization. The assessment to match this would not be a translation of the article, but would ask students to actually grapple with a new text and identify the gist of its content and some of the details that led to that identification.

Curriculum based on performance assessments remains flexible. Identifying performance assessment targets allows teachers to plan instruction based on personal knowledge and experience. What the students need to have in common in order to progress to the next level is not the exact same vocabulary or irregular verb forms, but rather a common level of performance. Even when students are in the same class experiencing the same instruction, they do not exit with the same recall of vocabulary or grammatical structures. When students come to the next level of instruction from a variety of teachers, expecting identical recall is unrealistic. Focusing on common performance targets and identifying how students will demonstrate progress toward them go a long way in helping students move from one course to the next without having to leap ahead, slow down, or feel lost.

Use Performance Assessments to Focus Curriculum Design

Once teachers identify clear performance targets that capture the goals for a course or level of instruction, they are ready to design curriculum. When district language teachers identify the essential performances for each course or level, they have a stronger framework for connecting their courses than one based on a sequence of grammar topics. By keeping their curriculum's clear performance goals in mind as they design instruction, teachers will develop effective activities and formative assessments to help students be successful in those summative performances. This is the essence of the backward design principles of Grant Wiggins and Jay McTighe[2]: identify clear performance goals, then create assessment tasks through which students will demonstrate the performance goals, and finally plan what students need to know and be able to do in

order to be successful in the assessments—that is, the vocabulary, grammatical items, and language functions.

Backward-designed curriculum, building from performance goals to performance assessments, provides teachers with the critical answer to the question of "how much" students need to know and when to stop. Without a clear idea of what students should be able to do as a result of the unit of instruction, the teacher will not know how much is enough and how much is too much to teach. With a clear assessment task in mind, teachers can identify the vocabulary items and structures required by the task.

Performance assessments provide a realistic description of expected student progress in developing proficiency in the language. The performances show what a Novice learner looks like compared to Intermediate and Pre-Advanced students. The curriculum development process needs to focus on critiquing the performance assessments to make sure that they are predictable and limited at the Novice level; that at the Intermediate level they require that students make their own choices and use language they know so as to get around language they do not know in order to be understood; and that at the Pre-Advanced level they require that students present a persuasive argument. These broad targets are described in greater detail in the *ACTFL Performance Guidelines for K–12 Learners*[3] (see Appendix B).

When a PK–12 or a postsecondary program's curriculum is based on performance assessments, the spiral nature of the curriculum can be made clear. The program curriculum should show the introduction of some specific language element (e.g., vocabulary, grammar, function); then the practice of that element and the gain of some manipulative ability; then the growing independent use of that element; and finally the "mastery" or fluent and less-conscious use of that element. The next step is to envision, develop, and implement performance tasks to check student progress along this continuum of learning, starting with formative learning checks and moving to end-of-unit assessments. This curriculum spiral is vastly different from a curriculum based on grammar items and discrete item vocabulary. Such a curriculum leads to discrete achievement testing, substituting knowledge *about* the language for knowledge to *use* the language.

Curriculum Example: Asking for Information

Level	Performance Target	Language Elements
Novice	Ask questions using a memorized pattern	Question words, tag questions
Intermediate-Weak	Offer a response in order to draw out the information needed	Phrases such as "tell me" and "would you please. . .?"
Intermediate-Strong	Re-state what was said and ask a follow-up question	Vocabulary for paraphrasing ("you mean to say that…")
Pre-Advanced	Probe and follow-up partner's comments, using different question structures	Connecting devices

Use Performance Assessment Feedback to Focus Design of Instructional Units and Daily Lessons

A powerful use of the performance assessment tasks is to provide feedback to the teacher. This feedback helps the teacher with the design of instructional units and daily lessons to focus on what students need to know. An analysis of the rubrics for the students in a class on an assessment task gives the teacher specific information on what to include in practice activities, direct instruction, or open-ended tasks in the next unit of instruction. If the rubrics reveal that students are weak in maintaining conversation by following up with comments or questions, the teacher can teach and practice specific strategies for doing so, and have students use them in formative assessment tasks in the next unit of instruction.

When students take ownership of identifying their learning goals (through strategies discussed in Chapter 5), they can help the teacher create the list of language skills they want to practice. The teacher can use the rubric for interpersonal tasks in the unit and ask students to add a blank row, then have each student write in a personal improvement goal area, such as asking follow-up questions. Then during pair activities and other interpersonal formative assessments, the teacher provides feedback on the categories designated for the whole class plus feedback on the individual learning target. In this way, feedback can easily be individualized. At the same time, this emphasis on feedback to the students will influence how the teacher designs daily lessons. The teacher will include elements of performance tasks that lead students to demonstrate the personalized categories on which they want feedback. Feedback becomes very personalized as each student receives information on specific individual learning goals.

With clear performance assessment tasks identified and with a curriculum based on these assessment tasks, teachers can focus the design of their units of instruction and daily lessons. Now the emphasis is on designing or adapting those activities that will best help students learn the curriculum elements in preparation for the performance assessment tasks that end the unit.

Getting Ready for an Integrated Performance Assessment[4]

Just as language learners require carefully planned and well-sequenced learning opportunities that provide practice in using the language in order to develop proficiency, they also need to know beforehand how they are going to be assessed and the kind of performance that is expected of them. In the language classroom it is important that learners know what targeted outcomes are for their level—what meets or exceeds expectations as well as what does not meet expectations for students at their level.

For example, the teacher might ensure that students know the expected outcomes at the end of the semester or year by providing in advance the rubrics for interpretive, interpersonal, and presentational communicative modes. The teacher might

---

Note: This chapter reproduces material directly from the Integrated Performance Assessment Manual. See Endnotes on p. 90 for page numbers.

Glisan, E., Adair-Hauck, B., Koda, K., Sandrock, P., & Swender, E. (2003). *ACTFL integrated performance assessment*. Alexandria, VA: The American Council on the Teaching of Foreign Languages.

also post the K–12 performance guidelines on the bulletin board for continuous reference. The classroom activities that take place during the year are focused on students being able to use their language in meaningful contexts based on the realistic expectations communicated to them.

Providing the rubrics and defining the performance expectations to students allows them to monitor their own progress, set realistic goals for themselves, and constantly work on improving their performance. In turn, students understand their roles and responsibilities in the language learning process. Students see the relevance and importance of assessment. As they envision the goals that they need to work toward, they become more independent language learners.

Assessment can improve performance if students have access to:
- the criteria and standards for the tasks they need to master
- feedback in the attempts to master the tasks
- opportunities to use the feedback to improve their performances[5]

Strategies to Prepare Students for the Interpretive Tasks[6]

In each IPA, students read, view, or listen to an authentic text related to the theme of the IPA. Students complete the interpretive task in the form of a "comprehension guide," which helps students to illustrate their level of comprehension and interpretation. The comprehension guide assesses the targeted level of performance as defined in the *ACTFL Performance Guidelines for K–12 Learners*. [See Appendixes B and C.]

The tasks within the guide are designed around an authentic text that is selected especially for performance at the Novice, Intermediate, or Pre-Advanced level. The tasks progress across levels, from those that require *literal comprehension*—detection of key words, main ideas, and supporting details—to more *interpretive comprehension*—identification of word and concept inferences, author/cultural perspectives, and the organizing principle(s) of the text. An important aspect of prepar-

ing students for these interpretive tasks is the selection of the appropriate level of text for both classroom practice and use in the IPA.

Selecting Appropriate Authentic Texts for the Interpretive Tasks[7]

The teacher can use various sources from the real world to find the text types required for the interpretive tasks, both for the classroom practice that leads up to the IPA and for the IPA itself. The texts selected must be authentic (i.e., prepared by and for native speakers of the target language). In order to maintain the integrity of the authentic text, teachers should not change the text in an attempt to simplify it for learners. Instead, the teacher should teach students strategies for understanding authentic texts such as using their background knowledge, guessing in context, and using word families to figure out the meaning of new words. (Note that while not always the case, the oral and printed texts included in standardized textbook programs are often prepared by textbook authors for instructional purposes and, therefore, cannot be considered authentic.)

Following are level-specific characteristics for authentic texts that can be used at each of the three levels of language proficiency. The levels are based on the *ACTFL Performance Guidelines for K–12 Learners*.

What to Look for When Selecting Novice-Level Authentic Texts for Interpretive Tasks[8]

The specific abilities being assessed at the Novice level are keyword recognition and main-idea detection. Most appropriate for the Novice level are:
- Short texts within highly predictable and familiar contexts related to personal experiences
- Selections that range in length from lists to simple sentences to more connected texts with loosely and highly predictably-ordered information
- Texts that are strongly supported by context, usually visual, with content of a frequent everyday nature

Sources of Novice-Level Texts for Interpretive Listening/Viewing Tasks	Sources of Novice-Level Texts for Interpretive Reading Tasks
• Simple interviews or surveys from a youth-oriented TV program based on the theme • Straightforward conversations taped from a youth-oriented music program on TV or radio • Highly contextualized product commercials in the target language from TV or radio • Highly contextualized public service announcements on radio or TV such as anti-smoking or anti-drug campaigns • Authentic songs by artists of the target culture based on familiar contexts or theme being studied	• Simple personal letters or e-mail correspondence • Simple biographies or descriptions of people from a popular culture magazine or newspaper • Highly contextualized product commercials in the target language from newspaper or magazines • Highly contextualized public service announcements in magazines and newspapers such as anti-smoking or anti-drug campaigns • Product advertisements or sales advertisements from a supermarket

What to Look for When Selecting Intermediate-Level Authentic Texts for Interpretive Tasks[9]

The specific abilities being assessed at the Intermediate level are detection of main ideas and supporting details. Word and concept inferences using contextual information are also targeted for those readers who may exceed expectations at the Intermediate level. Most appropriate for the Intermediate level are:

• Narratives, simple stories, routine correspondence, or other contextualized text (printed or audio or visual) within familiar contexts related to personal experience and background

• Information-packed texts (dense information) with a highly-predictable order of information

• Selections that range in length from simple sentences, to compound and/or complex sentences, to paragraph-like text

• Topics of high interest to students. Texts should contain cultural aspects of the target culture, which students can compare and contrast to those of their own culture (e.g., coming of age, health practices)

What to Look for When Selecting Pre-Advanced Level Authentic Texts for Interpretive Tasks[10]

The specific abilities being assessed at the Pre-Advanced level are: detection of main ideas and supporting details, word and concept inferences, identification of author/cultural perspectives, identification of organizing principle(s) of the text.

Most appropriate for the Pre-Advanced level are:

• Texts containing longer and more complex connected discourse

• Stories, narratives, social correspondence involving present, past, and future events

• Topics of personal and general interest

• Texts (fiction and nonfiction) covering a wide variety of topics found in the target culture, from popular media to literary texts

Sources of Intermediate-Level Texts for Interpretive Listening/Viewing Tasks	Sources of Intermediate-Level Texts for Interpretive Reading Tasks
• Highly contextualized product commercials in the target language from TV or radio • Highly contextualized public service announcements on TV or radio such as anti-smoking or anti-drug campaigns • Simple segments from soap operas or other TV programs • Simple, straightforward interviews from talk shows from the target cultures • Straightforward authentic songs by artists of the target culture based on the theme	• Highly contextualized product advertisements in the target language from newspaper or magazines • Highly contextualized public service announcements in magazines and newspapers such as anti-smoking or anti-drug campaigns • Interviews or surveys from youth-oriented magazines that deal with the theme being studied • Simple stories • Personal letters or e-mail correspondence regarding the theme • "Dear Abby"-type advice columns of personal interest to students • Photo stories with captions such as the "fotonovelas" that are very popular in Hispanic cultures

Sources of Pre-Advanced Level Texts for Interpretive Listening/Viewing Tasks	Sources of Pre-Advanced Level Texts for Interpretive Reading Tasks
• Contextualized comic strips and animated cartoons • Segments from soap operas or other TV programs • Interviews from talk shows from the target cultures • Interviews or surveys from youth-oriented magazines that deal with the theme being studied • Product commercials in the target language from newspapers or magazines • Public service announcements in magazines and newspapers such as anti-smoking or anti-drug campaigns	• Personal letters or e-mail correspondence regarding the theme • Photo stories with captions such as the "fotonovelas" that are very popular in Hispanic cultures • Authentic short stories by target culture authors • Essays or editorials in authentic target culture newspapers • Contextualized authentic songs or poetry by artists of the target culture • Contextualized comic strips from the target culture

Developing Interpretive Communication Skills in the Classroom[11]

Preparing students to comprehend and interpret an authentic text in the IPA requires a number of instructional strategies to give students confidence in dealing with the target language in its authentic form. Some strategies that the teacher might use include:

- Integrating authentic texts into instruction on a regular basis
- Providing opportunities for students to explore an authentic text in order to glean either the main idea or specific details (skimming or scanning), but without having to demonstrate an understanding of the entire text
- Preparing students for the task by activating their background knowledge and engaging them in anticipating the main idea of what they will listen to/read/view
- Encouraging students to develop their own purposes for listening to/reading/viewing an authentic text
- Providing students with strategies for comprehending authentic printed texts such as using contextual clues, using word families as clues to figuring out the meaning of new words, identifying key words that provide meaning clues, using titles and visuals that appear with the text as clues to meaning
- Providing students with strategies for comprehending authentic oral texts such as listening to the recorded segment a number of times each time for additional information, pausing the segment to give time for recalling what was heard, listening for key words only
- Designing interpretive activities that include pair and group collaboration
- Assisting students in moving from literal comprehension (key word, main idea and supporting-detail detection) to interpretive comprehension (word and concept inferences, author/cultural perspectives, organizational principles of the text)

- Providing opportunities for students to select their own authentic texts of interest and demonstrate their comprehension and interpretation of them

Strategies to Prepare Students for Interpersonal Tasks[12]

During an interpersonal task, two students exchange information with each other and express feelings, emotions, and opinions about the theme. Each of the two speakers comes to the task with information that the other person may not have, thereby creating an information gap, or a real need for students to provide and obtain information through the active negotiation of meaning. This exchange of information takes place spontaneously, without written support or notes.

Preparing students to engage in spontaneous conversation in the IPA requires a number of instructional strategies to help them develop communication tactics. Some strategies that the teacher might use include:

- Beginning with warm-up activities that lower the affective filter and provide students with planning time
- Providing students with pre-thinking exercises or graphic organizers to activate the thought process
- Providing students with videotaped models of interpersonal communication and engaging them in analysis of the models
- Weaning students from reliance on a written script or notes in their oral communication
- Providing multiple opportunities for students to practice "thinking on their feet" without the pressure of being evaluated constantly
- Providing students early on with conversational gambits in the target language as a means for negotiating meaning (e.g., "Could you repeat that please?" "Do you mean to say

that…?"); a list of these expressions could be displayed in the classroom for part of the year until students are able to use them without reference to the list

- Including as a regular classroom feature opportunities for the teacher to engage students in interpersonal communication on topics of school and individual interest, both with the teacher and with fellow classmates (e.g., opening of class when the teacher engages the class in sharing opinions about the upcoming basketball championship game)

- Integrating ongoing opportunities for students to ask questions in the target language within tasks where there is an information gap, thus motivating students to make inquiries for real-world purposes

- Including activities in which students communicate with one another on some aspects of an interpretive task done (e.g., an authentic reading or recorded segment)

- Providing opportunities for each student to interact with a variety of peers, some of whom may have language proficiency below the student while others may have the same or higher proficiency; this ensures students will at times assist lower-level students while at other times they are challenged by students at their own or higher levels

Strategies to Prepare Students for Presentational Tasks[13]

In a presentational task, students communicate a message to an audience of listeners or readers. Since the audience is not usually able to negotiate meaning with the creator of the message, presentational communication is referred to as one-way communication. In the IPAs, students communicate messages by means of products that include oral public service announcements, short speeches, written essays or letters, and written magazine articles. These products are often the culminating phase of the IPA and build upon the interpretive and interpersonal tasks.

The rubrics used to evaluate presentational communication include the use of the criterion called *impact*, which refers to the degree to which the message maintains the attention of the reader or listener. The teacher should explore with students strategies for creating presentational products that have impact (e.g., selection of topic, use of visuals, choice of words, visual layout).

Preparing students to perform presentational tasks in the IPA requires a number of instructional strategies to help them produce messages that are clear and that address the targeted audience. Some strategies that the teacher might use include:

- Creating presentational tasks so that they have a process-oriented approach, with phases for drafting, peer editing, revising, and rewriting

- Offering feedback to students that includes attention to the message itself in addition to linguistic accuracy

- Providing periodic opportunities for students to judge the impact of the presentational messages of others so that they become more familiar with this aspect of their work

- Providing periodic opportunities for students to share their work with audiences other than the teacher and receive feedback from them

- In the case of oral presentational communication, periodically recording student presentations and having students analyze their own work

With implementation of the types of strategies outlined in this section, the teacher should find a seamless connection between classroom practice and the IPA.

Impact of Performance Assessment on Classroom Instruction and Learning

The feedback received from teachers and students in ACTFL's IPA Project revealed the following types of impact of the project on instruction and learning:

- Using the IPA provided a way for teachers to integrate the standards into the classroom and allowed them to better understand the link between assessment and instruction. IPAs gave teachers a test toward which it was worth teaching.

- Teachers reported a better understanding of the three modes of communication and the relationship between the modes. Teachers learned how to create classroom instruction to help students perform better on the IPAs.

- Two-thirds of the teachers reported that they planned to make some significant changes to their instruction, or that the IPAs reinforced what they were already doing, reaffirmed their approach to instruction, and gave them encouragement to continue teaching for proficiency.

- Teachers said that they were ready to incorporate more interpersonal speaking tasks as assessments; integrate more authentic materials for class activities; utilize an integrated approach in their lesson design; explain the rubrics to their students at the beginning of the school year; set performance targets for their students; and continue to use video and authentic reading materials in their assessment.

- Teachers reported that the feedback sheets, which gave feedback based on the rubric criteria, were effective for students, and a timesaver for teachers. Teachers gave students productive comments that were consistent and constructive, avoiding non-descriptive words such as "nice" and "good."

- Some teachers expressed discomfort with not being able to easily convert rubrics into letter grades for their school districts, highlighting the depth of change that is required by performance assessments.

- Students generally felt challenged and successful. In their evaluation of the process, students found the IPA model to be engaging and motivating and asked for more assessments of this type.[14]

Develop District- or Department-Wide Performance Assessments Through an Ongoing Process of Review and Refinement

This process of designing performance assessments and using them to focus instruction is powerful for the individual teacher. For an entire department or district, it is transforming. One district[15] created summative performance assessment tasks for each of the three modes of communication (interpretive, interpersonal, and presentational) for each semester of the program. In the first year, they created assessment tasks only for the end of the first year. Teachers were asked to have their students do the assessment, but the district discussion was only based on their experience, not on the student results. The second year, teachers did the same with assessment tasks for the end of the first and second years of instruction. Teachers then brought three examples of the student work to a district-wide discussion: a strong performance, an average performance, and a weak performance. Sharing these examples helped the teachers to fine-tune their common goals and expectations, as well as to refine the tasks when the performances generated were not exactly what they wanted to see. Each year, teachers prepared performance assessments for the next level, in effect "growing" the performance assessments with the same group of students moving through the program year to year. This process reassured teachers that students were improving and

were showing increasing accuracy and sophistication in their use of the language.

By the end of this project, the teachers had identified common goals across all the languages taught in the district and targeted their expected performance for the end of the first semester of instruction, the second semester, and so on to the final semester of the program. The impact was tremendous. Conversation in the teachers' lounge moved from what chapter each teacher was on to how each was preparing students for their common assessments. The teachers noticed a huge shift from just teaching the curriculum to focusing on student learning, on how they could help students develop their language proficiency.

Another district used student data to shape its district program and smooth the articulation from middle school to high school.[16] For the design of its program of instruction in elementary grades, each unit of instruction connected to grade-level content, such as science units on the life cycle of the butterfly or social studies units on neighborhoods, was focused through specific performance assessments for each of the three modes of instruction (interpretive, interpersonal, and presentational). The program started with instruction in kindergarten and first grade. Each year the next grade level was added, in order to base the next year's performance targets and assessment tasks on the reality of what students were able to do in the language, not on a predetermined scope and sequence. The system worked through the end of middle school, adding performance targets each year.

When the first group of students entered eighth grade, the district faced the challenge of how to place them the next year into the existing high school program, a somewhat traditional sequence of five levels. Building on the success of their work developing district-wide performance assessments for grades K–8, the teachers decided to use the same approach for high school placement. They designed an interpersonal conversational task and a presentational writing task. All eighth grade students performed the two tasks, as did all high school students in first-year and second-year language courses. The interpersonal and presentational samples were evaluated with numbers rather than names to identify each student. Teachers rated each student as really good, OK, and weak. When the data was collected, the students were identified. To their surprise, the eighth grade students were generally in the "really good" pile, proving that they were at least as proficient in their performance as the second-year high school students, if not stronger. Based on this data, the decision was made to place all eighth grade students into the third-year high school course, knowing that even if they did not have all the specific vocabulary and grammatical knowledge of the current second-year students, they would be able to function at least as well as the current second-year students when they were mixed together in the third-year course.

The teachers then began to consider how it might be possible to move students to the next level based on proficiency rather than on seat time, knowing that even when students are in the same class the development of their proficiency may vary tremendously. Since the teachers were developing summative performance assessments for each unit of instruction, even in high school, they decided to continue to use this performance evidence to indicate when students were ready to move on to the next level. In cooperation with the high school administration and counselors, the process became formalized as follows: With the assessment data from each unit in a semester, the teachers identified those students who were consistently exceeding expectations on the assessment rubrics each semester. Since "Exceeds Expectations" for one level matched "Meets Expectations" of the next level, they knew that these students would function comfortably in the next level. The administration agreed that at any semester point, a student could move on to the next level, based on the assessment evidence. So, students might stay at the same level for one, two, three, or even four semesters. The decision was made to limit the length of time in one level to four semesters. To facilitate this, the teachers developed two years of units with different content, but focused on the same language targets; that is, the thematic focus changed with each unit over the four semesters, but the language elements being practiced were all geared to help the students move toward "Exceeds Expectations." Some students did move on after only one semester of instruction, most moved on after two semesters, and some students stayed on for a third or even a fourth semester of instruction at the same level. The advantage that teachers identified was that instead of having a huge range of proficiency in the same course

because all students were forced to move on at the end of the previous year or course, this way the students in each course were more similar in their proficiency, and thus the instruction could be targeted more effectively and efficiently to help all students move on to the next level.

The professional development based on designing and refining performance assessments brings the language department together. Based on the feedback from student results, teachers continue their discussion of learning targets, performance assessments, feedback mechanisms, and clear outcomes of learning activities. This is an ongoing process.

These processes for designing performance assessments show the power of identifying goals for a language department, describing how students will demonstrate those goals through actual performances, designing the tasks that will pull out the targeted performance, and providing feedback for both teachers and students to know the progress being made. Such a transparent and coherent assessment plan has numerous benefits:

1. Students are aware of the expectations and their progress toward meeting them.
2. Teachers focus on continuous student progress.
3. Students experience consistent goals throughout the language program.
4. Teachers collaborate on designing effective activities, since they are all working on the same unit and course goals.
5. Students are able to use the language that they are learning in meaningful contexts.
6. Teachers no longer hear former language students say, "I took two years of that language and I can't do a thing with it."

When student progress is measured through performance assessment and effective feedback, students know what they can do in the new language they are acquiring and what they need to do to improve their proficiency and increase their confidence in using the three modes of communication. This is the road map to guide language teaching and learning.

References

Chapter 1

Endnotes:

[1] Black, P., & Wiliam, D. (1998). Inside the black box: Raising standards through classroom assessment. *Phi Delta Kappan, 80*(2). 139–144, 146–148. Accessed at http://www.setda.org/toolkit/nlitoolkit2006/data/Data_InsideBlackBox.pdf on September 25, 2010. [Reference: p. 1.]

[2] Popham, J. (2008). *Transformative assessment.* Alexandria, VA: Association for Supervision and Curriculum Development. [Reference: p. 6.]

[3] Brookhart, S. (2004). *Grading.* Upper Saddle River, NJ: Pearson Education. [Reference: p. 45.]

Chapter 2

Endnotes:

[1] Glisan, E., Adair-Hauck, B., Koda, K., Sandrock, P., & Swender, E. (2003). *ACTFL integrated performance assessment.* Alexandria, VA: The American Council on the Teaching of Foreign Languages. Note: this chapter reproduces material directly from this manual's description of the Integrated Performance Assessment, pages 17–21, 24–26.

The Integrated Performance Assessment project is detailed in the following article:
Adair-Hauck, B., Glisan, E., Koda, K., Swender, E., & Sandrock, P. (2006). The integrated performance assessment (IPA): Connecting assessment to instruction and learning. *Foreign Language Annals, 39*(3), 359–382.

[2] Wiggins, G., & McTighe, J. (2005). *Understanding by design. Second edition.* Alexandria, VA: Association for Supervision and Curriculum Development.

[3] *ACTFL performance guidelines for K–12 learners.* (1998). Yonkers, NY: The American Council on the Teaching of Foreign Languages.

Chapter 3

Research Summary References (p. 12):

Adair-Hauck, B. & Cumo-Johanssen, P. (1997). Communication goal: Meaning making through a whole language approach. In J. K. Phillips (Ed.), *Collaborations: meeting new goals, new realities, Northeast Conference Reports* (pp. 35–96). Lincolnwood, IL: NTC/Contemporary Publishing Group.

Bloom, B. S. (Ed.). (1956). *Taxonomy of educational objectives: Classification of educational goals. Handbook 1: Cognitive domain.* New York: Longman, Green & Co.

Cummins, J. (1981). The role of primary language development in promoting educational success for language minority students. In *Schooling and language minority students: A theoretical framework.* Los Angeles: Evaluation, Dissemination, and Assessment Center, California State University.

Curtain, H., & Dahlberg, C. A. (2004). *Languages and children: Making the match* (3rd ed.). Boston: Pearson Education.

Gardner, H. (1991). *The unschooled mind: How children think and how schools should teach.* New York: Basic Books.

Geddes, M., & White, R. (1978). The use of semi-scripted simulated authentic speech in listening comprehension. *Audiovisual Language Journal, 16,* 137–145.

Hammadou Sullivan, J. A. (2002). Advanced foreign language readers' inferencing. In J. A. Hammadou Sullivan (Ed.), *Literacy and the second language learner* (pp. 217–238). Greenwich, CT: Information Age Publishing.

Herron, C., Corrie, C., Cole, s. P., & Dubreil, S. (1999). The effectiveness of a video-based curriculum in teaching culture. *The Modern Language Journal, 83,* 518–533.

Krashen, S. (1982). *Principles and practice in second language acquisition.* Oxford, UK: Pergamon Press.

Ramsay, R. (1991). French in action and the grammar question. *French Review, 65,* 255–266.

Rifkin, B. (2000). Video in the proficiency-based advanced conversation class: An example from the Russian-language curriculum. *Foreign Language Annals, 33,* 63–70.

Scarcella, R. C., & Oxford, R. L. (1992). *The tapestry of language learning.* Boston: Heinle & Heinle.

Shrum, J., & Glisan, E. (2005). *Teacher's handbook: Contextualized language instruction.* Boston, MA: Thomson Publishing, Heinle & Heinle.

Swaffar, J., Arens, K., & Byrnes, H. (1991). *Reading for meaning.* Englewood Cliffs, NJ: Prentice Hall.

Swain, M. (1985). Communicative competence: Some roles of comprehensible input and comprehensible output in its development. In S. Gass & C. Madden (Eds.), *Input in second language acquisition* (pp. 235–253). Rowley, MA: Newbury House.

Swain, M. (1995). Three functions of output in second language learning. In G. Cook & B. Seidlhofer (Eds.), *Principle and practice in applied linguistics: Studies in honour of H.G. Widdowson* (pp. 125–144). Oxford, UK: Oxford University Press.

Terry, R. M. (1998). Authentic tasks and materials for testing in the foreign language classroom. In J. Harper, M. Lively, & M. Williams (Eds.), *The coming of age of the profession* (pp. 277–290). Boston: Heinle & Heinle.

Toth, P. (2004). When grammar instruction undermines cohesion in L2 Spanish classroom discourse. *The Modern Language Journal, 88,* 14–30.

Vigil, V. D. (1987). Authentic text in the college-level Spanish I class as the primary vehicle of instruction. Unpublished doctoral dissertation. University of Texas, Austin.

Villegas Rogers, C., & Medley, Jr., F. W. (1988). Language with a purpose: Using authentic materials in the foreign language classroom. *Foreign Language Annals, 21,* 467–478.

Vogely, A. J. (1998). Listening comprehension anxiety: Students' reported scores and solutions. *Foreign Language Annals, 31,* 67–80.

Wiggins, G., & McTighe, J. (2005). *Understanding by design. Second edition.* Alexandria, VA: Association for Supervision and Curriculum Development.

Young, D. J. (1993). Processing strategies of foreign language readers: Authentic and edited input. *Foreign Language Annals, 26,* 451–468.

Young, D. J. (1999). Linguistic simplification of SL reading material: Effective instructional practice? *The Modern Language Journal, 83,* 350–366.

Endnotes:

[1] Curtain, H., & Dahlberg, C. (2004). *Languages and children: Making the match, new languages for young learners, Grades K–8 (3rd Edition).* Columbus, OH: Allyn & Bacon. [Reference: p. 147.]

[2] Glisan, E. (2009). Personal Communication.

[3] Wiggins, G., & McTighe, J. (2005). *Understanding by design. Second edition.* Alexandria, VA: Association for Supervision and Curriculum Development. [Reference: p. 342].

[4] Glisan, E. (2009). Personal Communication.

[5] Glisan, E. (2009). Personal Communication.

[6] Glisan, E. (2009). Personal Communication.

[7] Glisan, E. (2009). Personal Communication.

[8] National Standards in Foreign Language Education Project. (2006). *Standards for foreign language learning in the 21st century.* Lawrence, KS: Allen Press, Inc.

[9] Glisan, E. (2009). Personal Communication.

[10] Glisan, E. (2009). Personal Communication.

[11] Wiggins, G., & McTighe, J. (2005). *Understanding by design. Second edition.* Alexandria, VA: Association for Supervision and Curriculum Development.

[12] Curtain, H. (2006). Keynote presentation. Pacific Northwest Council for Languages.

[13] McTighe, J., & Ferrara, S. (1998). *Assessing learning in the classroom.* Washington, DC: National Education Association. [Reference: p. 12]. Note: several examples were added by the author, with some adaptation of the chart.

[14] Clementi, D., & Sandrock, P. (2005). Workshop materials, building on K–12 Performance Guidelines.

[15] Based on tasks from Sandrock, P. (2002). *Planning curriculum for learning world languages.* Madison, WI: Department of Public Instruction. [Reference: p. 35].

[16] Contribution of Lynn Sessler (Clovis Grove Elementary School, Menasha, WI), featured in *World language assessment: Get in the mode!* produced by Educational Communications Board, Madison, WI. Accessed at http://www.ecb.org/worldlanguageassessment/ on September 25, 2010.

[17] Sandrock, P. (2002). *Planning curriculum for learning world languages.* Madison, WI: Department of Public Instruction. Selected thematic curriculum units from Chapter 4.

[18] Sandrock, P. (2002). *Planning curriculum for learning world languages.* Madison, WI: Department of Public Instruction. [Reference: p. 4.]

Chapter 4

Research Summary References (p. 36):

Bachman, L. F. (1990). *Fundamental considerations in language testing.* Oxford, UK: Oxford University Press.

Bacon, S. M. (1992). Phases of listening to authentic input in Spanish: A descriptive study. *Foreign Language Annals, 25,* 317–334.

Campbell, R., & Wales, R. (1970). The study of language acquisition. In J. Lyons (Ed.), *New horizons in linguistics* (pp. 242–260). Harmondsworth, England: Penguin.

Canale, M., & Swain, M. (1980). Theoretical bases of communicative approaches to second language teaching and testing. *Applied Linguistics, 1,* 1–47.

Celce-Murcia, M., Dörnyei, Z., & Thurrell, S. (1995). Communicative competence: A pedagogically motivated model with content specifications. *Issues in Applied Linguistics, 6,* 5–35.

Cohen, A. D. (1987). Student processing of feedback on their compositions. In A. Wenden & J. Rubin (Eds.), *Learner strategies in language learning* (pp. 57–68). Englewood Cliffs, NJ: Prentice Hall.

Cohen, A. D., & Cavalcanti, M. C. (1990). Feedback on compositions: Teacher and student verbal reports. In B. Kroll (Ed.), *Second language writing: Research insights for the classroom* (pp. 155–177). Cambridge, UK: Cambridge University Press.

Coombs, V. M. (1986). Syntax and communicative strategies in intermediate German composition. *The Modern Language Journal, 70,* 114–124.

Doughty, C., & Pica, T. (1986). Information gap tasks: Do they facilitate acquisition? *TESOL Quarterly, 20,* 315–326.

Ferris, D. R. (2003). Responding to writing. In B. Kroll (Ed.), *Exploring the dynamics of second language writing* (pp. 119–140). Cambridge, UK: Cambridge University Press.

Frantzen, D. (1995). The effects of grammar supplementation on written accuracy in an intermediate Spanish course. *The Modern Language Journal, 79,* 324–344.

Hymes, D. (1972). On communicative competence. In J. P. Pride & J. Holmes (Eds.), *Sociolinguistics* (pp. 269–293). Harmondsworth, UK: Penguin.

Porter, P. A. (1986). How learners talk to each other: Input and interaction in task-centered discussions. In R. R. Day (Ed.), *Talking to learn: Conversation in second language acquisition* (pp. 200–224). Rowley, MA: Newbury House.

Savignon, S. J. (1972). *Communicative competence: An experiment in foreign language teaching.* Philadelphia: Center for Curriculum Development.

Semke, H.D. (1984). Effects of the red pen. *Foreign Language Annals, 17,* 195–202.

Shrum, J. & Glisan, E. (2005). *Teacher's handbook: Contextualized language instruction.* Boston, MA: Thomson Publishing, Heinle & Heinle.

Vygotsky, L. S. (1978). *Mind in society: The development of higher psychological processes.* Cambridge, MA: Harvard University Press.

Endnotes:

[1] Commodore, C. (1992). Assessment strategies. Heartland AEA (workshop handout).

[2] The author first learned the phrase "non-negotiables" in the context of assessment as used in this publication from Donna Clementi through collaboration developing workshops on assessment.

[3] Clementi, D. (2000). Personal Communication.

[4] Gorski, S. (2008). Personal Communication.

[5] New Jersey participants in an IPA workshop conducted by the author created this summary of the *ACTFL Performance Guidelines for K–12 Learners* (2003).

[6] For more information on LinguaFolio, a project of the National Council of State Supervisors for Languages (NCSSFL): http://www.ncssfl.org/links/index.php?linguafolio. For the "Can Do" statements: http://www.ncssfl.org/links/LFGrid.pdf.

[7] Concordia Language Villages. (2010). *The Explorer journal.* Moorhead, MN: Concordia Language Villages. [Based on the Concordia Language Visa, a LinguaFolio NCSSFL project. Reference: pp. 52-65].

[8] Concordia Language Villages. (2010). *The Explorer journal.* Moorhead, MN: Concordia Language Villages. [Based on the Concordia Language Visa, a LinguaFolio NCSSFL project. Reference: pp. 52-65].

[9] Gifford, C. & Mullaney, J. (2002). Oral assessments–Novice level. In *Professional development module V: Developing rubrics for performance-based assessment.* Cox, D., & Dunn, B. Austin, TX: Languages Other Than English Center for Educator Development, Southwest Educational Development Laboratory. [Used with permission, reference: p. C–13].

[10] Clementi, D. and Sandrock, P. (2005). Workshop materials.

[11] Commodore, C. (2009). Personal Communication.

Chapter 5

Research Summary References (p. 68):

Donato, R. (2004). Collective scaffolding. In J. Lantolf & G. Appel (Eds.), *Vygotskyan approaches to second language acquisition research* (pp. 35–56). Norwood, NJ: Ablex.

Donato R., & McCormick, D. (1994). A sociocultural perspective on language learning strategies: The role of mediation. *The Modern Language Journal, 78,* 453–464.

Dörnyei, Z. (1994). Motivation and motivating in the foreign language classroom. *The Modern Langauge Journal, 78,* 273–284.

Gardner, R. C. (1985). *Social psychology and second language learning: The role of attitudes and motivation.* London, Ontario, Canada: Edward Arnold.

Johnson, D., & Johnson, R. (1987). *Learning together and alone: Cooperation, competition, and individualization.* Englewood Cliffs, NJ: Prentice Hall.

Lapkin, S., Swain, M., & Smith, M. (2002). Reformulation and the learning of French pronominal verbs in a Canadian French immersion context. *The Modern Language Journal, 86,* 485–507.

Masgoret, A.-M., & Gardner, R. C. (2003). Attitudes, motivation, and second language learning: A meta-analysis of studies conducted by Gardner and Associates. *Language Learning, 53,* 123–163.

McCafferty, S. G. (2002). Gesture and creating zones of proximal development for second language learning. *The Modern Language Journal, 86,* 192–203.

Oxford, R., & Shearin, J. (1994). Language learning motivation: Expanding the theoretical framework. *The Modern Language Journal, 78,* 12–28.

Shrum, J. & Glisan, E. (2005). *Teacher's handbook: Contextualized language instruction.* Boston, MA: Thomson Publishing, Heinle & Heinle.

Wen, X. (1997). Motivation and language learning with students of Chinese. *Foreign Language Annals, 30,* 235–251.

Endnotes:

[1] Sandrock, P. (2002). *Planning curriculum for learning world languages.* Madison, WI: Wisconsin Department of Public Instruction.

[2] Glisan, E., Adair-Hauck, B., Koda, K., Sandrock, P., & Swender, E. (2003). *ACTFL integrated performance assessment.* Alexandria, VA: The American Council on the Teaching of Foreign Languages. [This section is excerpted from pp. 12–15].

[3] Vygotsky, L. S. (1978). *Mind in society: The development of higher psychological processes.* (M. Cole, V. John-Steiner, S. Scribner, & El. Souberman, Eds. & Trans.). Cambridge, MA: Harvard University Press. [Reference: p. 86].

[4] Vygotsky, L. S. (1986). *Thought and language, Revised edition.* Alex Kozulin, Ed. Cambridge, MA: The Massachusetts Institute of Technology Press. [Reference: p. 278]. (Note: italics in original)

[5] Tharp, R. & R. Gallimore. (1988). *Rousing minds to life: Teaching, learning and schooling in social contexts.* Cambridge, MA: Cambridge University Press.

[6] Adair-Hauck, B. and R. Donato. 1994. Foreign language explanations within the zone of proximal development. *Canadian Modern Language Review, 50,* 532–557.

[7] Tharp and Gallimore, 1988, p. 60.

[8] Tharp and Gallimore, 1988, p. 59.

Chapter 6

Research Summary References (p. 78):

Blythe, T., Allen, D., & Schieffelin, B. (2007). *Looking together at student work, Second edition.* New York: Teachers College Press.

Goddard, Y. L., Goddard, R. D., & Tschannen-Moran, M. (2007). A theoretical and empirical investigation of teacher collaboration for school improvement and student achievement in public elementary schools. *Teachers College Record, 109*(4), 877–896.

Herman, R., Dawson, P., Dee, T., Greene, J., Maynard, R., Redding, S., & Darwin, M. (2008). Turning around chronically low-performing schools: A practice guide (NCEE #2008-4020). Washington, D.C.: U.S. Department of Education, Institute of Education Sciences, National Center for Education Evaluation and Regional Assistance. Accessed at http://ies.ed.gov/ncee/wwc/practiceguides on September 25, 2010.

Horn, I. (2006). Teacher collaboration and ambitious teaching: Reflections on what matters. *New Horizons for Learning*. Accessed at http://www.newhorizons.org/spneeds/inclusion/staff/horn.htm on September 25, 2010.

Endnotes:

[1] Sandrock, P. This was the author's experience as a ninth grade teacher of Spanish (Appleton Area School District, Wisconsin), which led to a districtwide project to share more communicative assessment strategies.

[2] Wiggins, G., & McTighe, J. (2005). *Understanding by design. Second edition.* Alexandria, VA: Association of Supervision and Curriculum Development.

[3] *ACTFL performance guidelines for K–12 learners.* (1998). Yonkers, NY: The American Council on the Teaching of Foreign Languages.

[4] Glisan, E., Adair-Hauck, B., Koda, K., Sandrock, P., & Swender, E. (2003). *ACTFL integrated performance assessment.* Alexandria, VA: The American Council on the Teaching of Foreign Languages, pp. 26–27.

[5] Wiggins, G. (1998). *Educative assessment.* San Francisco: Jossey-Bass.

[6] Glisan, et. al. *ACTFL integrated performance assessment*, p. 27

[7] Glisan, et. al. *ACTFL integrated performance assessment*, pp. 27–28

[8] Glisan, et. al. *ACTFL integrated performance assessment*, p. 28

[9] Glisan, et. al. *ACTFL integrated performance assessment*, p. 29

[10] Glisan, et. al. *ACTFL integrated performance assessment*, p. 30

[11] Glisan, et. al. *ACTFL integrated performance assessment*, pp. 30–31

[12] Glisan, et. al. *ACTFL integrated performance assessment*, pp. 31–32

[13] Glisan, et. al. *ACTFL integrated performance assessment*, pp. 32–33

[14] Glisan, et. al. *ACTFL integrated performance assessment*, pp. 15–16

[15] Clementi, D. The Appleton Area School District (WI) undertook a project to create common assessments for each semester in the six-year language sequence.

[16] Sessler, L. The Menasha Joint School District (WI) undertook this project to create its K–12 program based on agreed-upon standards-based assessments to chart student progress on all three modes of communication.

Appendix A

National Standards for Foreign Language Learning

National Standards in Foreign Language Education Project. (2006). *Standards for foreign language learning in the 21ˢᵗ century.* (3rd ed.) Lawrence, KS: Allen Press.

Communication

Communicate in Languages Other Than English

Standard 1.1: Students engage in conversations, provide and obtain information, express feelings and emotions, and exchange opinions.

Standard 1.2: Students understand and interpret written and spoken language on a variety of topics.

Standard 1.3: Students present information, concepts, and ideas to an audience of listeners or readers on a variety of topics.

Cultures

Gain Knowledge and Understanding of Other Cultures

Standard 2.1: Students demonstrate an understanding of the relationship between the practices and perspectives of the culture studied.

Standard 2.2: Students demonstrate an understanding of the relationship between the products and perspectives of the culture studied.

Connections

Connect with Other Disciplines and Acquire Information

Standard 3.1: Students reinforce and further their knowledge of other disciplines through the foreign language.

Standard 3.2: Students acquire information and recognize the distinctive viewpoints that are only available through the foreign language and its cultures.

Comparisons

Develop Insight into the Nature of Language and Culture

Standard 4.1: Students demonstrate understanding of the nature of language through comparisons of the language studied and their own.

Standard 4.2: Students demonstrate understanding of the concept of culture through comparisons of the cultures studied and their own.

Communities

Participate in Multilingual Communities at Home and Around the World

Standard 5.1: Students use the language both within and beyond the school setting.

Standard 5.2: Students show evidence of becoming life-long learners by using the language for personal enjoyment and enrichment.

Appendix B

ACTFL Performance Guidelines for K–12 Learners

American Council on the Teaching of Foreign Languages. (1999). *ACTFL performance guidelines for K-12 learners*. Yonkers, NY: ACTFL.

NOVICE LEARNER RANGE
(Grade K–4, Grade 5–8, Grade 9–10)

COMPREHENSIBILITY: How well are they understood?

Interpersonal

- Rely primarily on memorized phrases and short sentences during highly predictable interactions on very familiar topics;
- Are understood primarily by those very accustomed to interacting with language learners;
- Imitate modeled words and phrases using intonation and pronunciation similar to that of the model;
- May show evidence of false starts, prolonged and unexpectedly-placed pauses and recourse to their native language as topics expand beyond the scope of immediate needs;
- Are able to meet limited practical writing needs, such as short messages and notes, by recombining learned vocabulary and structure to form simple sentences on very familiar topics.

Presentational

- Use short, memorized phrases and sentences in oral and written presentations;
- Are understood primarily by those who are very accustomed to interacting with language learners;
- Demonstrate some accuracy in pronunciation and intonation when presenting well-rehearsed material on familiar topics;
- May show evidence of false starts, prolonged and unexpectedly-placed pauses, and recourse to their native language as topics expand beyond the scope of immediate needs;
- Show abilities in writing by reproducing familiar material
- Rely heavily on visuals to enhance comprehensibility in both oral and written presentations.

COMPREHENSION: How well do they understand?

Interpersonal

- Comprehend general information and vocabulary when the communication partner uses objects, visuals, and gestures in speaking or writing;
- Generally need contextual clues, redundancy, paraphrase or restatement in order to understand the message.

Interpretive

- Understand short, simple conversations and narratives (live and recorded material), within highly predictable and familiar contexts;
- Rely on personal background experience to assist in comprehension;
- Exhibit increased comprehension when constructing meaning through recognition of key words or phrases embedded in familiar contexts;
- Comprehend written and spoken language better when content has been previously presented in an oral and/or visual context;
- Determine meaning by recognition of cognates, prefixes, and thematic vocabulary.

LANGUAGE CONTROL: How accurate is their language?

Interpersonal

- Comprehend messages that include predominately familiar grammatical structures;
- Are most accurate when communicating about very familiar topics using memorized oral and written phrases;
- Exhibit decreased accuracy when attempting to create with the language;
- Write with accuracy when copying written language but may use invented spelling when writing words or producing characters on their own;
- May exhibit frequent errors in capitalization and punctuation when target language differs from native language in these areas.

Interpretive

- Recognize structural patterns in target language narratives and derive meaning from these structures within familiar contexts;
- Sometimes recognize previously learned structures when presented in new contexts.

Presentational

- Demonstrate some accuracy in oral and written presentations when reproducing memorized words, phrases and sentences in the target language;
- Formulate oral and written presentations using a limited range of simple phrases and expressions based on very familiar topics;
- Show inaccuracies and/or interference from the native language when attempting to communicate information which goes beyond the memorized or pre-fabricated;
- May exhibit frequent errors in capitalization and/or punctuation and/or production of characters when the writing system of the target language differs from the native language.

VOCABULARY USE: How extensive and applicable is their vocabulary?

Interpersonal

- Comprehend and produce vocabulary that is related to everyday objects and actions on a limited number of familiar topics;
- Use words and phrases primarily as lexical items without awareness of grammatical structure;
- Recognize and use vocabulary from a variety of topics including those related to other curricular areas;
- May often rely on words and phrases from their native language when attempting to communicate beyond the word and/or gesture level.

Interpretive

- Recognize a variety of vocabulary words and expressions related to familiar topics embedded within relevant curricular areas;
- Demonstrate increased comprehension of vocabulary in spoken passages when these are enhanced by pantomime, props, and/or visuals;
- Demonstrate increased comprehension of written passages when accompanied by illustrations and other contextual clues.

Presentational

- Use a limited number of words and phrases for common objects and actions in familiar categories;
- Supplement their basic vocabulary with expressions acquired from sources such as the teacher or picture dictionaries;
- Rely on native language words and phrases when expressing personal meaning in less familiar categories.

COMMUNICATION STRATEGIES: How do they maintain communication?

Interpersonal

- Attempt to clarify meaning by repeating words and occasionally selecting substitute words to convey their message;
- Primarily use facial expressions and gestures to indicate problems with comprehension.

Interpretive

- Use background experience to anticipate story direction in highly predictable oral or written texts;
- Rely heavily on visuals and familiar language to assist in comprehension.

Presentational

- Make corrections by repeating or rewriting when appropriate forms are routinely modeled by the teacher;
- Rely heavily on repetition, non-verbal expression (gestures, facial expressions), and visuals to communicate their message.

CULTURAL AWARENESS: How is their cultural understanding reflected in their communication?

Interpersonal

- Imitate culturally appropriate vocabulary and idiomatic expressions;
- Use gestures and body language that are generally those of the student's own culture, unless they are incorporated into memorized responses.

Interpretive

- Understand both oral and written language that reflects a cultural background similar to their own;
- Predict a story line or event when it reflects a cultural background similar to their own.

Presentational

- Imitate the use of culturally appropriate vocabulary, idiomatic expressions and non-verbal behaviors modeled by the teacher.

INTERMEDIATE LEARNER RANGE

COMPREHENSIBILITY: How well are they understood?

Interpersonal

- Express their own thoughts using sentences and strings of sentences when interacting on familiar topics in present time;
- Are understood by those accustomed to interacting with language learners;
- Use pronunciation and intonation patterns which can be understood by a native speaker accustomed to interacting with language learners;
- Make false starts and pause frequently to search for words when interacting with others;
- Are able to meet practical writing needs, such as short letters and notes, by recombining learned vocabulary and structures demonstrating full control of present time and evidence of some control of other time frames.

Presentational

- Express their own thoughts, describe and narrate, using sentences and strings of sentences, in oral and written presentations on familiar topics;
- Use pronunciation and intonation patterns that can be understood by those accustomed to interacting with language learners;
- Make false starts and pause frequently to search for words when interacting with others;
- Communicate oral and written information about familiar topics with sufficient accuracy that listeners and readers understand most of what is presented.

COMPREHENSION: How well do they understand?

Interpersonal

- Comprehend general concepts and messages about familiar and occasionally unfamiliar topics;
- May not comprehend details when dealing with unfamiliar topics;
- May have difficulty comprehending language supported by situational context.

Interpretive

- Understand longer, more complex conversations and narratives as well as recorded material in familiar contexts;

- Use background knowledge to comprehend simple stories, personal correspondence, and other contextualized print;
- Identify main ideas and some specific information on a limited number of topics found in the products of the target culture such as those presented on TV, radio, video or live and computer-generated presentations, although comprehension may be uneven;
- Determine meaning by using contextual clues;
- Are aided by the use of redundancy, paraphrase, and restatement in order to understand the message.

LANGUAGE CONTROL: How accurate is their language?

Interpersonal

- Comprehend messages that include some unfamiliar grammatical structures;
- Are most accurate when creating with the language about familiar topics in present time using simple sentences and/or strings of sentences;
- Exhibit a decline in grammatical accuracy as creativity in language production increases;
- Begin to apply familiar structures to new situations;
- Evidence awareness of capitalization and/or punctuation when writing in the target language;
- Recognize some of their own spelling or character production errors and make appropriate adjustments.

Interpretive

- Derive meaning by comparing target language structures with those of the native language;
- Recognize parallels between new and familiar structures in the target language;
- Understand high-frequency idiomatic expressions.

Presentational

- Formulate oral and written presentations on familiar topics, using a range of sentences and strings of sentences primarily in present time but also, with preparation, in past and future time.
- May show inaccuracies as well as some interference from the native language when attempting to present less familiar material;
- Exhibit fairly good accuracy in capitalization and punctuation (or production of characters) when target language differs from native language in these areas.

VOCABULARY USE: How extensive and applicable is their vocabulary?

Interpersonal

- Use vocabulary from a variety of thematic groups;
- Recognize and use vocabulary from a variety of topics including those related to other curricular areas;
- Show some understanding and use of common idiomatic expressions;
- May use false cognates or resort to their native language when attempting to communicate beyond the scope of familiar topics.

Interpretive

- Comprehend an expanded range of vocabulary;
- Frequently derive meaning of unknown words by using contextual clues;
- Demonstrate enhanced comprehension when listening to or reading content which has a recognizable format.

Presentational

- Demonstrate control of an expanding number of familiar words and phrases and of a limited number of idiomatic expressions;
- Supplement their basic vocabulary, for both oral and written presentations, with expressions acquired from other sources such as dictionaries;
- In speech and writing, may sometimes use false cognates and incorrectly applied terms, and show only partial control of newly acquired expressions.

COMMUNICATION STRATEGIES: How do they maintain communication?

Interpersonal

- May use paraphrasing, question-asking, circumlocution, and other strategies to avoid a breakdown in communication;
- Attempt to self-correct primarily for meaning when communication breaks down.

Interpretive

- Identify the main idea of a written text by using reading strategies such as gleaning information from the first and last paragraphs;
- Infer meaning of many unfamiliar words that are necessary in order to understand the gist of an oral or written text;
- Use contextual clues to assist in comprehension.

Presentational

- Make occasional use of reference sources and efforts at self-correction to avoid errors likely to interfere with communication;
- Use circumlocution when faced with difficult syntactic structures, problematic spelling, or unfamiliar vocabulary;
- Make use of memory aids (such as notes and visuals) to facilitate presentations.

CULTURAL AWARENESS: How is their cultural understanding reflected in their communication?

Interpersonal

- Use some culturally appropriate vocabulary and idiomatic expressions;
- Use some gestures and body language of the target culture.

Interpretive

- Use knowledge of their own culture and that of the target culture(s) to interpret oral or written texts more accurately;
- Recognize target culture influences in the products and practices of their own culture;
- Recognize differences and similarities in the perspectives of the target culture and their own.

Presentational

- Use some culturally appropriate vocabulary, idiomatic expressions and non-verbal behaviors;
- Demonstrate some cultural knowledge in oral and written presentations.

PRE-ADVANCED LEARNER RANGE (Grade K–12)

COMPREHENSIBILITY: How well are they understood?

Interpersonal

- Narrate and describe using connected sentences and paragraphs in present and other time frames when interacting in topics of personal, school, and community interest;
- Are understood by those with whom they interact, although there may still be a range of linguistic inaccuracies, and on occasion the communication partner may need to make a special effort to understand the message;

- Use pronunciation and intonation patterns that are understandable to a native speaker unaccustomed to interacting with language learners;
- Use language confidently and with ease, with few pauses;
- Are able to meet practical writing needs such as letters and summaries by writing descriptions and narrations of paragraph length and organization, showing sustained control of basic structures and partial control of more complex structures and time frames.

Presentational

- Report, narrate and describe, using connected sentences, paragraph-length and longer discourse, in oral and written presentations on topics of personal, school, and community interest;
- Use pronunciation and intonation patterns that are understood by native users of the language, although the listener/reader may on occasion need to make a special effort to understand the message;
- Use language confidently and with ease, with few pauses;
- Communicate with a fairly high degree of facility when making oral and written presentations about familiar and well-researched topics.

COMPREHENSION: How well do they understand?

Interpersonal

- Comprehend main ideas and most details on a variety of topics beyond the immediate situation;
- Occasionally do not comprehend but usually are able to clarify details by asking questions;
- May encounter difficulty comprehending language dealing with abstract topics.

Interpretive

- Use knowledge acquired in other settings and from other curricular areas to comprehend both spoken and written messages;
- Understand main ideas and significant details on a variety of topics found in the products of the target culture such as those presented on TV, radio, video or live and computer-generated presentations, although comprehension may be uneven;
- Develop an awareness of tone, style and author perspective;
- Demonstrate a growing independence as a reader or listener and generally comprehend what they read and hear without relying solely on formally learned vocabulary.

LANGUAGE CONTROL: How accurate is their language?

Interpersonal

- Comprehend messages that include unfamiliar grammatical structures;
- Are most accurate when narrating and describing in connected sentences and paragraphs in present time with decreasing accuracy in past and future times;
- May continue to exhibit inaccuracies as the amount and complexity of language increases;
- Communicate successfully by applying familiar structures to new situations;
- Rarely make errors in capitalization and in punctuation;
- Are generally accurate in spelling or production of characters.

Interpretive

- Deduce meaning in unfamiliar language passages by classifying words or concepts according to word order or grammatical use;
- Apply rules of language to construct meaning from oral and written texts;
- Understand idiomatic expressions;
- Move beyond literal comprehension toward more critical reading and listening.

Presentational

- Accurately formulate paragraph-length and longer oral and written presentations in present time, on topics of personal, school, community and global interest;
- May show some inaccuracies and/or interference from the native language when presentations deal with multiple time frames and/or other complex structures;
- Successfully communicate personal meaning by applying familiar structures to new situations and less familiar topics, and by integrating information from audio, visual, and written sources;
- Exhibit awareness of need for accuracy in capitalization and/or punctuation (or production of characters) when target language differs from native language in these areas.

VOCABULARY USE: How extensive and applicable is their vocabulary?

Interpersonal

- Understand and often use idiomatic and culturally authentic expressions;

- Recognize and use vocabulary from a variety of topics including those related to other curricular areas;
- Use more specialized and precise vocabulary terms within a limited number of topics.

Interpretive

- Comprehend a wide range of vocabulary in both concrete and abstract contexts;
- Infer meaning of both oral and written texts by recognizing familiar words and phrases in new contexts;
- Use context to deduce meaning of unfamiliar vocabulary;
- Recognize and understand the cultural context of many words and phrases.

Presentational

- Demonstrate control of an extensive vocabulary, including a number of idiomatic and culturally authentic expressions, from a variety of topics;
- Supplement their basic vocabulary by using resources such as textbooks and dictionaries;
- May use more specialized and precise terms when dealing with specific topics that have been researched.

COMMUNICATION STRATEGIES: How do they maintain communication?

Interpersonal

- Are able to sustain an interaction with a native speaker by using a variety of strategies when discussion topics relate to personal experience or immediate needs;
- Show evidence of attention to mechanical errors even when these may not interfere with communication.

Interpretive

- Use background knowledge to deduce meaning and to understand complex information in oral or written texts;
- Identify the organizing principle(s) or oral or written texts;
- Infer and interpret the intent of the writer.

Presentational

- Demonstrate conscious efforts at correct formulation and self-correction by use of self-editing and of reference sources;
- Sustain length and continuity of presentations by appropriate use of strategies such as simplification, reformulation, and circumlocution;
- Make use of a variety of resource materials and presentation methods to enhance presentations.

CULTURAL AWARENESS: How is their cultural awareness reflected in their communication?

Interpersonal

- Use culturally appropriate vocabulary and idioms;
- Use appropriate gestures and body language of the target culture.

Interpretive

- Apply understanding of the target culture to enhance comprehension of oral and written texts;
- Recognize the reflections of practices, products, and/or perspectives of the target cultures(s) in oral and written texts;
- Analyze and evaluate cultural stereotypes encountered in oral and written texts.

Presentational

- Demonstrate increased use of culturally appropriate vocabulary, idiomatic expressions and non-verbal behaviors;
- Use language increasingly reflective of authentic cultural practices and perspectives.

Appendix C | IPA Comprehension Guide Templates

Glisan, E., Adair-Hauck, B., Koda, K., Sandrock, P., & Swender, E. (2003). *ACTFL integrated performance assessment.* Alexandria, VA: American Council on the Teaching of Foreign Languages.

Novice Level

I. **Key word recognition.**

Find in the article the Spanish/French/German word that best expresses the meaning of each of the following English words:

_____   _____

_____   _____

_____   _____

_____   _____

II. **Important words and phrases.**

Note to teacher: Provide 5 correct ideas and 3 distracters.

First, circle the letter of the ideas mentioned in the article.
Then, write the letter of that idea next to where it appears in the text.

A. _____

B. _____

C. _____

D. _____

E. _____

F. _____

G. _____

H. _____

III. **Main idea(s).**

Using information from the article, provide the main idea(s) of the article in English.

_____

_____

Intermediate Level

I.   **Main idea(s).**

Using information from the article, provide the main idea(s) of the article in English.

_____

_____

II. **Supporting details.** For each of the following,

- circle the letter of each detail that is mentioned in the article
- write the information that is given in the article in the space provided next to the detail below

Note to teacher: Provide 5 correct statements that support the main idea(s) and 3 distracters.

A. _____

B. _____

C. _____

D. _____

E. _____

F. _____

G. _____

H. _____

III. **Meaning from context.**

Based on this passage write what the following three words probably mean in English.

Note to teacher: Provide three words that the student may not be likely to know but will be able to understand from the context.

1. _____

2. _____

3. _____

IV. **Inferences.**

Answer the following questions by providing as many reasons as you can. Your responses may be in English or in _____ .

Note to teacher: Write two open-ended questions "why do you think that", "why is it important that", "what might be the effect of", etc., that require inference on the part of the student.

1. Question: _____

Use details from the article to support your answer.

2. Question: _____

Explain.

Pre-Advanced Level

I. **Main idea(s).**

Using information from the article, provide the main idea(s) of the article in English.

_____

_____

II. **Supporting details.** For each of the following,
- circle the letter of each detail that is mentioned in the article
- write the information that is given in the article in the space provided next to the detail below

Note to teacher: Provide 5 correct statements that support the main idea(s) and 3 distracters.

A. _____

B. _____

C. _____

D. _____

E. _____

F. _____

G. _____

H. _____

III. **Meaning from context.**

Based on this passage write what the following three words probably mean in English.

Note to teacher: Provide three words that the student may not be likely to know but will be able to understand from the context.

1. _____

2. _____

3. _____

IV. **Concept inferences.** "Read between the lines" in order to answer, in English, the following questions:

Note to teacher: Create questions that require students to infer the author's intent.

1. _____

2. _____

3. _____

Pre-Advanced Level (continued)

V.   **Author's perspective.** Circle the letter of the perspective or point of view you think the author adopted as s/he wrote this article and justify your answer with information from the text.

Note to teacher: Provide one correct answer and two distracters. Possible options may include clinical/ scientific, moral/religious, humanistic, factual/historical, comic, etc.)

A.   _____

B.   _____

C.   _____

Justification from text: _____

VI.   **Comparing cultural perspectives.** Answer the following question in English:

Note to teacher: Here are some possible types of questions:

What are the cultural similarities and differences between _____ and _____ ?

How do the practices/products in the article reflect the target culture perspectives?

What did you learn about the target culture from this article?

How would this article have been different if it were written for a U.S. audience?

VII.   **Personal reaction to the text.** Using specific information from the text, describe your personal reaction to the article. Be sure to provide reasons that support your reaction.*

VIII.   **Organizing principle.** How is this article organized? Circle all that apply.

A.   Chronological order

B.   Pros and cons

C.   Cause/effect

D.   Compare/contrast

E.   Story telling

F.   Problem and solution

*Note to teacher: Due to the personalized nature of this item, the response is not evaluated in the rubrics.

Appendix D

Integrated Performance Assessment (IPA) Rubrics

Glisan, E., Adair-Hauck, B., Koda, K., Sandrock, P., & Swender, E. (2003). *ACTFL integrated performance assessment.* Alexandria, VA: American Council on the Teaching of Foreign Languages.

Interpretive Rubric–Novice Learner

Text types: short narratives within highly predictable and familiar contexts related to personal experiences

Interpretive	Exceeds Expectations*	Meets Expectations	Does Not Meet Expectations
Literal Comprehension:			
Word recognition		Recognizes key words or phrases.	Recognizes a few key words or phrases.
Main idea detection		Identifies most or significant important ideas expressed in words or phrases embedded in familiar contexts.	Identifies a few important ideas expressed in words or phrases embedded in familiar contexts.
Supporting detail detection		Identifies the main idea(s) of the Novice-level text.	Does not identify the main idea(s) of the Novice-level text.
Interpretive Comprehension:			
Word inferences			
Concept inferences			
Author/cultural			
Perspectives			
Organizational principles			

* Note: Due to the limited nature of the text type used for Novice learners, performance beyond "Meets Expectations" is not assessed in the current version of the IPA.

Interpretive Rubric–Intermediate Learner

Text types: longer, more detailed conversations and narratives, simple stories, correspondence and other contextualized print within familiar contexts

Interpretive	Exceeds Expectations*	Meets Expectations	Does Not Meet Expectations
Literal Comprehension:			
Word recognition			Recognizes key words or phrases embedded in familiar contexts.
Main idea detection		Identifies the main idea(s) of the Intermediate-level text.	Does not identify the main idea(s) of the Intermediate-level text.
Supporting detail detection	Identifies most supporting details.	Identifies some supporting details.	Identifies few supporting details.
Interpretive Comprehension:			
Word inferences	Infers meaning of unfamiliar words in new contexts.		
Concept inferences	Infers and interprets the author's intent.		
Author/cultural			
Perspectives			
Organizational principles			

* At the Intermediate level, the learner exceeds expectations by performing both the literal and the interpretive comprehension criteria.

Interpretive Rubric–Pre-Advanced Learner

Text types: longer, more complex connected discourse on a wide variety of topics found in the target culture, from popular media to literary texts

Interpretive	Exceeds Expectations*	Meets Expectations	Does Not Meet Expectations
Literal Comprehension:			
Word recognition			
Main idea detection		Identifies the main idea(s) of the Intermediate-level text.	Does not identify the main idea(s) of the Intermediate-level text.
Supporting detail detection	Identifies most supporting details.	Identifies most supporting details.	Identifies some supporting details.
Interpretive Comprehension:			
Word inferences	Infers meaning of unfamiliar words in new contexts.	Infers meaning of some unfamiliar words in new contexts.	Infers meaning of few unfamiliar words in new contexts.
Concept inferences	Infers and interprets the author's intent.	Infers and interprets some of the author's intent.	Does not infer or interpret the author's intent.
Author/cultural	Identifies the author's perspectives.	Identifies some of the author's perspectives.	Does not identify the author's perspectives.
Perspectives	Identifies cultural perspectives.	Identifies some cultural perspectives.	Does not identify cultural perspectives.
Organizational principles		Identifies the organizing principle(s) of the text.	Does not identify the organizing principle(s) of the text.

*At the Pre-Advanced level, the learner exceeds expectations by performing both the literal and the interpretive comprehension criteria.

Interpersonal Mode Rubric–Novice Learner

Category	Exceeds Expectations	Meets Expectations	Does Not Meet Expectations
Language Function Language tasks the student is able to handle in a consistent, comfortable, sustained, and spontaneous manner	Creates with language, able to express own meaning in a basic way.	Mostly memorized language with some attempts to create.	Memorized language only, familiar language.
Text Type Quantity and organization of language discourse (continuum: word–phrase–sentence–connected sentences–paragraph)	Simple sentences and some strings of sentences.	Simple sentences and memorized phrases.	Words, phrases, chunks of language, and lists.
Communication Strategies *Quality of engagement and interactivity*; amount of negotiation of meaning; how one participates in the conversation and advances it	Maintains simple conversation: asks and answers some basic questions (but still may be reactive).	Responds to basic direct questions. Asks a few formulaic questions (primarily reactive).	Responds to a limited number of formulaic questions (primarily reactive).
Clarification Strategies How the student handles a breakdown in comprehension; what one does when one partner doesn't understand the other	Clarifies by asking and answering questions.	Clarifies by occasionally selecting substitute words.	Clarifies meaning by repeating words and/or using English.
Comprehensibility Who can understand this person's meaning? How sympathetic must the listener be? Does it need to be the teacher or could a native speaker understand the speaker? How independent of the teaching situation is the conversation?	Generally understood by those accustomed to interacting with language learners.	Understood with occasional difficulty by those accustomed to interacting with language learners.	Understood primarily by those very accustomed to interacting with language learners.
Language Control Accuracy, form, appropriate vocabulary, degree of fluency	Most accurate when producing simple sentences in present time. Accuracy decreases as language becomes more complex.	Most accurate with memorized language, including phrases. Accuracy decreases when creating, when trying to express own meaning.	Most accurate with memorized language only. Accuracy may decrease when attempting to communicate beyond the word level.

Interpersonal Mode Rubric–Intermediate Learner

Category	Exceeds Expectations	Meets Expectations		Does Not Meet Expectations
		STRONG	**WEAK**	
Language Function Language tasks the student is able to handle in a consistent, comfortable, sustained, and spontaneous manner	Language expands toward narration and description that includes connectedness, cohesiveness, and different time frames.	Creates with language; ability to express own meaning expands in quantity and quality.	Creates with language, able to express own meaning in a basic way.	Mostly memorized language with some attempts to create.
Text Type Quantity and organization of language discourse (continuum: word–phrase–sentence–connected sentences–paragraph)	Mostly connected sentences and some paragraph-like discourse.	Strings of sentences; some connected sentence-level discourse (with cohesive devices), some may be complex (multi-clause) sentences.	Simple sentences and some strings of sentences.	Simple sentences and memorized phrases.
Communication Strategies *Quality of engagement and interactivity*; amount of negotiation of meaning; how one participates in the conversation and advances it	Initiates and maintains conversation using a variety of strategies.	Maintains conversation by asking and answering questions.	Maintains simple conversation: asks and answers some basic questions (but still may be reactive).	Responds to basic direct questions. Asks a few formulaic questions (primarily reactive).
Clarification Strategies How the student handles a breakdown in comprehension; what one does when one partner doesn't understand the other	Clarifies by paraphrasing.	Clarifies by asking and answering questions.	Clarifies by asking and answering questions.	Clarifies by occasionally selecting substitute words.
Comprehensibility Who can understand this person's meaning? How sympathetic must the listener be? Does it need to be the teacher or could a native speaker understand the speaker? How independent of the teaching situation is the conversation?	Although there may be some confusion about the message, generally understood by those unaccustomed to interacting with language learners.	Generally understood by those accustomed to interacting with language learners.	Generally understood by those accustomed to interacting with language learners.	Understood with occasional difficulty by those accustomed to interacting with language learners.
Language Control Accuracy, form, appropriate vocabulary, degree of fluency	Most accurate with connected discourse in present time. Accuracy decreases when narrating and describing in time frames other than present.	Most accurate with connected sentence-level discourse in present time. Accuracy decreases as language becomes more complex.	Most accurate when producing simple sentences in present time. Accuracy decreases as language becomes more complex.	Most accurate with memorized language, including phrases. Accuracy decreases when creating, when trying to express own meaning.

Interpersonal Mode Rubric–Pre-Advanced Learner

Category	Exceeds Expectations	Meets Expectations	Does Not Meet Expectations
Language Function Language tasks the student is able to handle in a consistent, comfortable, sustained, and spontaneous manner	Consistently and extensively narrates and describes in all major time frames.	Language expands toward narration and description that includes connectedness, cohesiveness, and different time frames.	Creates with language; ability to express own meaning expands in quantity and quality.
Text Type Quantity and organization of language discourse (continuum: word–phrase–sentence–connected sentences–paragraph)	Connected sentences and a predominance of paragraphs.	Mostly connected sentences and some paragraph-like discourse.	Strings of sentences, some connected sentence level discourse (with cohesive devices), some may be complex (multi-clause) sentences.
Communication Strategies *Quality of engagement and interactivity*; amount of negotiation of meaning; how one participates in the conversation and advances it	Initiates, advances, and/or redirects conversation.	Initiates and maintains conversation using a variety of strategies.	Maintains conversation by asking and answering questions.
Clarification Strategies How the student handles a breakdown in comprehension; what one does when one partner doesn't understand the other	Uses a wide variety of clarification strategies.	Clarifies by paraphrasing.	Clarifies by asking and answering questions.
Comprehensibility Who can understand this person's meaning? How sympathetic must the listener be? Does it need to be the teacher or could a native speaker understand the speaker? How independent of the teaching situation is the conversation?	Easily understood by native speakers, even those unaccustomed to interacting with language learners. Clear evidence of culturally appropriate language.	Although there may be some confusion about the message, generally understood by those unaccustomed to interacting with language learners.	Generally understood by those accustomed to interacting with language learners.
Language Control Accuracy, form, appropriate vocabulary, degree of fluency	High degree of accuracy in present, past and future time. Accuracy may decrease when attempting to handle abstract topics.	Most accurate with connected discourse in present time. Accuracy decreases when narrating and describing in time frames other than present.	Most accurate with connected sentence-level discourse in present time. Accuracy decreases as language becomes complex.

Presentational Mode Rubric–Novice Learner

Category	Exceeds Expectations	Meets Expectations	Does Not Meet Expectations
Language Function Language tasks the student is able to handle in a consistent, comfortable, sustained, and spontaneous manner	Creates with language, able to express own meaning in a basic way.	Mostly memorized language with some attempts to create.	Memorized language only, familiar language.
Text Type Quantity and organization of language discourse (continuum: word–phrase–sentence–connected sentences–paragraph)	Simple sentences and some strings of sentences.	Simple sentences and memorized phrases.	Words, phrases, chunks of language, and lists.
Impact Depth of presentation and attention to audience Vocabulary	Provides continuity to a presentation. Begins to make choices of a phrase, image, or content to maintain the attention of the audience. Vocabulary is sufficient to provide information and limited explanation.	Focuses on successful task completion. Uses gestures or visuals to maintain audience's attention and/or interest as appropriate to purpose. Vocabulary conveys basic information.	Presented in an unclear and/or unorganized manner. No effort to maintain audience's attention. Vocabulary is limited and/or repetitive.
Comprehensibility Who can understand this person's message? How sympathetic must the listener/reader be? Does it need to be the teacher or could a native speaker understand the message? How independent of the teaching situation is the presentation?	Generally understood by those accustomed to the speaking/writing of language learners.	Understood with occasional straining by those accustomed to the speaking/writing of language learners.	Understood primarily by those very accustomed to the speaking/writing of language learners.
Language Control Accuracy, form, degree of fluency	Most accurate when producing simple sentences in present time. Accuracy decreases as language becomes more complex.	Most accurate with memorized language, including phrases. Accuracy decreases when creating, when trying to express own meaning.	Most accurate with memorized language only. Accuracy may decrease when attempting to communicate beyond the word level.

Presentational Mode Rubric–Intermediate Learner

Category	Exceeds Expectations	Meets Expectations		Does Not Meet Expectations
		STRONG	WEAK	
Language Function Language tasks the student is able to handle in a consistent, comfortable, sustained, and spontaneous manner	Language expands toward narration and description that includes connectedness, cohesiveness, and different time frames.	Creates with language; ability to express own meaning expands in quantity and quality.	Creates with language, able to express own meaning in a basic way.	Mostly memorized language with some attempts to create.
Text Type Quantity and organization of language discourse (continuum: word–phrase–sentence–connected sentences–paragraph)	Mostly connected sentences and some paragraph-like discourse.	Strings of sentences; some connected sentence-level discourse (with cohesive devices), some may be complex (multi-clause) sentences	Simple sentences and some strings of sentences.	Simple sentences and memorized phrases.
Impact Depth of presentation and attention to audience Vocabulary	Provides continuity to a presentation. Makes choices of a phrase, image, or content to maintain the attention of the audience. Vocabulary provides information and limited explanation.	Provides continuity to a presentation. Begins to make choices of a phrase, image, or content to maintain the attention of the audience. Vocbulary is sufficient to provide information and limited explanation.	Provides continuity to a presentation. Begins to make choices of a phrase, image, or content to maintain the attention of the audience. Vocabulary is sufficient to provide information and limited explanation.	Focuses on successful task completion. Uses gestures or visuals to maintain audience's attention and/or interest as appropriate to purpose . Vocabulary conveys basic information.
Comprehensibility Who can understand this person's message? How sympathetic must the listener/reader be? Does it need to be the teacher or could a native speaker understand the message? How independent of the teaching situation is the presentation?	Although there may be some confusion about the message, generally understood by those unaccustomed to the speaking/writing of language learners.	Generally understood by those unaccustomed to the speaking/writing of language learners.	Generally understood by those accustomed to the speaking/writing of language learners.	Understood with occasional straining by those accustomed to the speaking/writing of language learners.
Language Control Accuracy, form, degree of fluency	Most accurate with connected discourse in present time. Accuracy decreases when narrating and describing in time frames other than present.	Most accurate with connected sentence-level discourse in present time. Accuracy decreases as language becomes more complex.	Most accurate when producing simple sentences in present time. Accuracy decreases as language becomes more complex.	Mostly accurate with memorized language, including phrases. Accuracy decreases when creating, when trying to express own meaning.

Presentational Mode Rubric–Pre-Advanced Learner

Category	Exceeds Expectations	Meets Expectations	Does Not Meet Expectations
Language Function Language tasks the student is able to handle in a consistent, comfortable, sustained, and spontaneous manner	Consistently and extensively narrates and describes in all major time frames.	Language expands toward narration and description that includes connectedness, cohesiveness, and different time frames.	Creates with language, ability to express own meaning expands in quantity and quality.
Text Type Quantity and organization of language discourse (continuum: word–phrase–sentence–connected sentences–paragraph)	Connected sentences and a predominance of paragraphs.	Mostly connected sentences and some paragraph-like discourse.	Strings of sentences, some connected sentence level discourse (with cohesive devices), some may be complex (multi-clause) sentences.
Impact Depth of presentation and attention to audience Vocabulary	Provides continuity to a presentation; compares and/or contrasts to reinforce the message. Motivates audience to keep reading/listening; personalizes to maintain or re-engage audience. Vocabulary effectively conveys information and elaborates.	Provides continuity to a presentation Makes choices of a phrase, image, or content to maintain the attention of the audience. Vocabulary provides information and limited explanation.	Provides continuity to a presentation. Begins to make choices of a phrase, image, or content to maintain the attention of the audience. Vocabulary is sufficient to provide information and limited explanation.
Comprehensibility Who can understand this person's message? How sympathetic must the listener/reader be? Does it need to be the teacher or could a native speaker understand the message? How independent of the teaching situation is the presentation?	Easily understood by native speakers, even those unaccustomed to the speaking/writing of language learners. Clear evidence of culturally appropriate language.	Although there may be some confusion about the message, generally understood by those unaccustomed the speaking/writing of language learners.	Generally understood by those accustomed to the speaking/writing of language learners.
Language Control Accuracy, form, degree of fluency	High degree of accuracy in present, past and future time. Accuracy may decrease when attempting to handle abstract topics.	Most accurate with connected discourse in present time. Accuracy decreases when narrating and describing in time frames other than present.	Most accurate with connected sentence-level discourse in present time. Accuracy decreases as language becomes more complex.

Appendix E

LinguaFolio Wisconsin: Culture

Wisconsin Association for Language Teachers (2007, pp. 22-23) http://www.waflt.org

Level: Beginning	I can do this somewhat	I can do this well	This is my goal
I can imitate or demonstrate appropriate patterns of behavior such as greetings and gestures with other people.			
I can do or explain many culture activities such as games, songs, and holiday celebrations.			
I can identify some major contributions and historical figures from the culture(s).			
I can identify countries, regions, and geographic features where the target language is spoken.			
Level: Developing	I can do this somewhat	I can do this well	This is my goal
I can interact with respect using culturally appropriate patterns of behavior in everyday informal and social situations.			
I can explain or discuss cultural and social activities common to a student my own age such as holiday celebrations, school life, and pastimes.			
I can identify some historical and contemporary influences from the culture(s) that impact today's society, such as democratic form of government and environmental concerns.			
I can explain the impact of the target country's geography on daily life.			
Level: Transitioning	I can do this somewhat	I can do this well	This is my goal
I can interact with respect according to the social and cultural requirements and most social and some formal contexts.			
I can compare and contrast activities from the culture(s) to my own culture in relation to home, school, community and nation.			
I can discuss how historical and contemporary influences from the culture(s) shape people's view of the world and my own attitudes towards issues facing the world.			
I can explain the impact of the target country's geography on the people's beliefs, perspectives, and attitudes.			
Level: Refining	I can do this somewhat	I can do this well	This is my goal
I can interact in a variety of context (formal/informal, social/work) with sensitivity and respect.			
I can discuss the role and importance of various social activities within the cultures studies, such as religious celebrations, historical events, and rites of passage.			
I can explain the impact of the culture's views on what is happening and could happen in the world today.			
I can evaluate the target country's geography with respect to the impact on politics, economics, and history.			

Appendix F | Proficiency Levels Needed in the World of Work

Proficiency Levels Needed in the World of Work

K-12 Performance Guidelines	Proficiency Level (OPI)	Functions	Corresponding Jobs/ Professions	Who has this level of proficiency?
	Superior	*Discuss topics extensively, support opinions and hypothesize. Deal with a linguistically unfamiliar situation*	Interpreter, accountant, executive, lawyer, judge, financial advisor	Educated native speakers; students from abroad after a number of years working in a professional environment
	Advanced-High	*Narrate and describe in past, present and future and deal effectively with an unanticipated complication*	University professor of foreign languages	Students with master's degrees or doctorates
	Advanced-Mid		Doctor, sales representative, social worker	Native speakers who learned Spanish in the home environment
	Advanced-Low		Customer service representatives, police officers, school teachers	Graduates with Spanish degrees who have lived in Spanish-speaking countries
Pre-Advanced	Intermediate-High	*Create with language, initiate, maintain and bring to a close simple conversations by asking and responding to simple questions*	Aviation personnel, telephone operator, receptionist	Graduates with Spanish degrees who have not lived in Spanish-speaking countries
Intermediate	Intermediate-Mid		Tour guide, cashier	After six years of middle/ high school, AP
	Intermediate-Low			After four years of high school
Novice	Novice-High	*Communicate minimally with formulaic and rote utterances, lists and phrases*		
	Novice-Mid			After two years of high school
	Novice-Low			

From the paper *La Enseñanza de Español y Otras Lenguas Extranjeras en los Estados Unidos: Cantidad y Calidad* (*The Teaching of Spanish and Other Foreign Languages in the United States: Quantity and Quality*) presented at the II Congreso de la Lengua Española in Valladolid, Spain, October 18, 2001 by Dr. Elvira Swender of the American Council on the Teaching of Foreign Languages (ACTFL)

NOTES:

1. The levels indicated are minimal proficiency levels for specific job descriptions and have been established by subject matter experts from a variety of agencies, organizations and companies for whom ACTFL provides oral proficiency testing following an analysis of the linguistic tasks and the responsibilities of the positions.

2. The references to how long it takes to reach certain levels of proficiency were written specifically for the study of Spanish, a Category I language. Other Category I languages include Afrikaans, Danish, Dutch, French, Haitian Creole, Italian, Norwegian, Portuguese, Romanian, Swahili and Swedish. For Category II, III and IV languages, one can expect that it will take longer to reach the same levels of proficiency.

Appendix G

LinguaFolio: Self-Assessment Grid

National Council of State Supervisors for Languages (2009) http://www.ncssfl.org

Interpretive

	Novice		
	Low	**Mid**	**High**
Listening	I can understand a few familiar words. I can understand some words that are similar to those in my own language.	I can understand some everyday words, phrases, and questions about me, my personal experiences, and my surroundings, when people speak slowly and clearly or there is repetition.	I can understand some ideas on familiar topics containing phrases, simple sentences, and frequently used expressions. I can understand the main point in short conversations, messages, and announcements.
Reading	I can identify some words, phrases, or characters, especially those that are similar to words in my own language.	I can understand familiar words, phrases, and simple sentences.	I can understand some ideas in simple texts that contain familiar vocabulary.

Interpersonal

	Novice		
	Low	**Mid**	**High**
Person to Person Communication	I can communicate using single words and memorized phrases.	I can interact with help using words, phrases, and memorized expressions. I can answer simple questions on very familiar topics.	I can exchange information on familiar tasks, topics, and activities. I can handle short social interactions using phrases and simple sentences, but I may need help or visuals to keep the conversation going.

Presentational

	Novice		
	Low	**Mid**	**High**
Spoken Production	I can provide information about myself and my immediate surroundings using single words or memorized phrases.	I can provide information about myself and my immediate surroundings using words, phrases, and memorized expressions.	I can provide basic information on familiar topics using phrases and simple sentences.
Written Production	I can copy some characters and words.	I can provide some basic information on familiar topics in lists, phrases, and memorized expressions.	I can write descriptions and short messages to request or provide information on familiar topics using phrases and simple sentences.

Interpretive

	Intermediate		
	Low	**Mid**	**High**
Listening	I can understand the main idea and some details on familiar topics expressed in sentences, short conversations, presentations, and messages.	I can understand the main idea and many details on familiar topics in a series of connected sentences, conversations, presentations, and messages.	I can understand the main points and most details in conversations, presentations, and messages on familiar topics. I can understand the main idea and some details on unfamiliar topics.
Reading	I can understand the main idea and some details in texts that contain familiar vocabulary.	I can understand the main idea and many details in texts that contain familiar vocabulary and some details in texts that contain unfamiliar vocabulary.	I can understand the main idea and most details in texts on familiar topics. I can understand the main idea and many details in texts that contain unfamiliar vocabulary.

Interpersonal

	Intermediate		
	Low	**Mid**	**High**
Person to Person Communication	I can begin and carry on a conversation on a limited number of familiar topics. I can ask and answer simple questions and exchange information in familiar situations using phrases and a series of sentences.	I can state my views and carry on conversations on a variety of familiar topics and in uncomplicated situations.	I can state and support many of my views and take an active part in discussions. I can handle some complicated situations on familiar topics.

Presentational

	Intermediate		
	Low	**Mid**	**High**
Spoken Production	I can provide information on familiar topics using a series of sentences with some details.	I can describe experiences, events, and plans, give opinions, narrate a story, and make a simple factual presentation using connected sentences with many details.	I can present information on familiar topics with clarity and detail. I can present my viewpoint on an issue and support my opinions.
Written Production	I can write on familiar topics and experiences using a series of sentences with some details.	I can write communications, descriptions, and explanations on familiar topics using connected sentences with many details.	I can write communications, narratives, descriptions, or explanations on familiar topics using connected, detailed paragraphs.

Interpretive

Advanced				Superior
	Low	**Mid**	**High**	
Listening	I can understand some extended speech on unfamiliar topics delivered through a variety of media.	I can understand most spoken language and some technical discussions. I can understand some accents and dialects.	I can clearly understand extended speech and short lectures, even when somewhat complicated. I can understand most forms of media with little effort.	I can understand any kind of spoken language, including most accents and dialects.
Reading	I can usually understand viewpoints and attitudes expressed in literary and nonliterary texts.	I can easily understand long, complex texts and recognize some literary and technical styles.	I can understand abstract and linguistically complex texts. I can make appropriate inferences and identify literary elements.	I can understand with ease virtually all forms of written language.

Interpersonal

Advanced				Superior
	Low	**Mid**	**High**	
Person to Person Communication	I can communicate with a fair amount of fluency and spontaneity on familiar topics, even in complicated situations. I can link ideas in extended discussions. I can participate actively in most informal and a few formal conversations.	I can actively express myself with fluency and flexibility on a range of familiar and some new topics, including concrete social, academic, and professional topics. I can express and defend my viewpoint or recommendations.	I can express myself with fluency, flexibility, and precision on concrete and some abstract topics. I can adapt my language in most situations.	I can effectively and consistently use language for all purposes. I can take part effortlessly in any conversation or discussion.

Presentational

Advanced				Superior
	Low	**Mid**	**High**	
Spoken Production	I can deliver a clear, organized presentation appropriate to my audience on a variety of topics.	I can deliver a clearly articulated presentation on personal, academic, or professional topics.	I can deliver a clear and fluid presentation and appropriately respond to the audience.	I can deliver a presentation for a variety of purposes in a style appropriate to any type of audience.
Written Production	I can express ideas on a variety of topics in clear, organized texts. I can adjust my writing for some audiences.	I can write detailed texts on a broad variety of concrete social and professional topics.	I can express myself with fluency and precision on concrete and some abstract topics. I can adapt my writing style according to purpose and audience.	I can effectively and consistently express myself in a variety of styles for academic and professional audiences and purposes.

* The Novice, Intermediate, Advanced, Superior designations represent approximations with the *ACTFL Proficiency Guidelines*.

Appendix H

IPA Project Acknowledgments

Glisan, E., Adair-Hauck, B., Koda, K., Sandrock, P., & Swender, E. (2003). *ACTFL integrated performance assessment*. Alexandria, VA: American Council on the Teaching of Foreign Languages, pp. 4-5.

Editors and Authors of Integrated Performance Assessment Manual

Eileen W. Glisan, Lead Editor
Indiana University of Pennsylvania, Indiana, PA

Bonnie Adair-Hauck
University of Pittsburgh, Pittsburgh, PA

Keiko Koda
Carnegie Mellon University, Pittsburgh, PA

S. Paul Sandrock
Wisconsin Department of Instruction, Madison, WI

Elvira Swender
American Council on the Teaching of Foreign Languages, Yonkers, NY

Acknowledgments

Standards Assessment Design Project Task Force

Elvira Swender, American Council on the Teaching of Foreign Languages, Project Director
S. Paul Sandrock, Wisconsin Department of Instruction, Project Coordinator
Bonnie Adair-Hauck, University of Pittsburgh, Pittsburgh, PA
Eileen Glisan, Indiana University of Pennsylvania, Indiana, PA
Keiko Koda, Carnegie Mellon University, Pittsburgh, PA
Michael Stewart, Standard & Poors, New York, NY

Pilot Site Coordinators

Martha G. Abbott, Fairfax County Public Schools, VA
Peggy Boyles, Putnam City Schools, OK
Donna Clementi, Appleton West High School, WI
Deborah Lindsay, Greater Albany School District, OR
Frank Mulhern, Wallingford-Swarthmore Schools, PA
Kathleen Riordan, Springfield Public Schools, MA

Assessment Fellows at Pilot Sites

Rosa Alvaro-Alves, Springfield Public Schools, MA
Linda Bahr, Greater Albany School District, OR
Carolyn Carroll, Fairfax County Public Schools, VA
Christine Carroll, Putnam City Schools, OK
Kathy Ceman, Butte des Morts Elementary, WI
Donna Clementi, Appleton West High School, WI
Karin Cochran, Jesuit High School, OR
Michele de Cruz-Sainz, Wallingford-Swarthmore School District, PA
Margaret Draheim, Appleton East High School, WI

Cathy Etheridge, Appleton East High School, WI

Carmen Felix-Fournier, Springfield Public Schools, MA

Catherine Field, Greater Albany School District, OR

Stephen Flesher, Beaverton Public Schools, OR

Nancy Gadbois, Springfield Public Schools, MA

Frederic Gautzsch, Wallingford-Swarthmore School District, PA

Susana Gorski, Nicolet Elementary School, WI

Susan Harding, Putnam City Schools, OK

Heidi Helmich, Madison Middle School, WI

Mei-Ju Hwang, Springfield Public Schools, MA

Betty Ivich, Putnam City Schools, OK

Michael Kraus, Putnam City Schools, OK

Irmgard Langacker, Wallingford-Swarthmore School District, PA

Dorothy Lavigne, Wallingford-Swarthmore School District, PA

Deborah Lindsay, Greater Albany School District, OR

Conrad Lower, Wallingford-Swarthmore School District, PA

Linda S. Meyer, Appleton North High School, WI

Paula J. Meyer, Appleton North High School, WI

Linda Moore, Putnam City Schools, OK

Frank Mulhern, Wallingford-Swarthmore School District, PA

Rita Oleksak, Springfield Public Schools, MA

Frances Pettigrew, Fairfax County Public Schools, VA

Rebecca Rowton, Rollingwood Elementary School, OK

Ann Smith, Jesuit High School, OR

Dee Dee Stafford, Putnam City Schools, OK

Adam Stryker, Fairfax County Public Schools, VA

Catherine Thurber, Tigard High School, OR

Ghislaine Tulou, Fairfax County Public Schools, VA

Carter Vaden, Fairfax County Public Schools, VA

Sally Ziebell, Putnam City Schools, OK

Special Acknowledgments to:

Everett Kline, CLASS, Pennington, NJ

Greg Duncan, InterPrep Inc., Marietta, GA

A Special Thank You to the Students of:

Albany High School, Albany, OR

Appleton Area Public Schools, WI

Beaverton Public Schools, OR

Fairfax County Public Schools, VA

Putnam City Public Schools, OK

Public Schools of Springfield, MA

Wallingford-Swarthmore Schools, PA

The Standards Assessment Design Project and the ACTFL Integrated Performance Assessments were funded under a grant from the U.S. Department of Education—International Research and Studies Program.

Notes:

Notes:

Notes: